COMPLEX PTSD WORKBOOK FOR WOMEN 5 IN 1

Heal Childhood Trauma, Overcome Emotional Triggers, and Build Lasting Resilience with Evidence-Based Therapies and Daily Recovery Tools

VIVIAN WHITMORE

© Copyright 2025. Vivian Whitmore. All rights reserved.

The content contained within this book may not be reproduced, duplicated or transmitted without direct written permission from the author or the publisher.

Under no circumstances will any blame or legal responsibility be held against the publisher, or author, for any damages, reparation, or monetary loss due to the information contained within this book, either directly or indirectly.

Legal Notice:
This book is copyright protected. It is only for personal use. You cannot amend, distribute, sell, use, quote or paraphrase any part, or the content within this book, without the consent of the author or publisher.

Disclaimer Notice:
Please note the information contained within this document is for educational and entertainment purposes only. All effort has been executed to present accurate, up to date, reliable, complete information. No warranties of any kind are declared or implied. Readers acknowledge that the author is not engaged in the rendering of legal, financial, medical or professional advice. The content within this book has been derived from various sources. Please consult a licensed professional before attempting any techniques outlined in this book.

By reading this document, the reader agrees that under no circumstances is the author responsible for any losses, direct or indirect, that are incurred as a result of the use of the information contained within this document, including, but not limited to, errors, omissions, or inaccuracies.

Table Of Contents

Book One
UNDERSTANDING AND BREAKING FREE FROM C-PTSD

Introduction 7
Chapter One: Understanding Complex Ptsd—Symptoms And Causes 9
Chapter Two: Childhood Trauma And Its Lasting Effects—A Feminine Perspective 17
Chapter Three: Trauma's Impact On Relationships, Self-Esteem, And Motherhood................29
Chapter Four: Breaking The Cycle—Tools For Awareness And Healing 39
Chapter Five: Deepening Your Understanding Of C-Ptsd 49
Conclusion..63

Book Two
Emotional Regulation And Management

Introduction 67
Chapter One: The Importance Of Emotional Regulation In Trauma Recovery........................69
Chapter Two : Identifying Triggers—A Woman's Journey 79
Chapter Three: Practical Techniques For Managing Anxiety And Overwhelm 93
Chapter Four: Creating An Emotional Self-Care Toolbox 103
Chapter Five: Receiving Emotional Support From Others 115
Conclusion..123

Book Three
Managing C-Ptsd Through Professional Therapeutic Techniques

Introduction	127
Chapter One: Introduction To Cognitive Processing Therapy	129
Chapter Two: Identifying Negative Core Beliefs	137
Chapter Three: Reframing Exercises—Healing Childhood Wounds	147
Chapter Four: Incorporating Other Therapeutic Approaches—A Holistic View	159
Chapter Five: Additional Exercises—CBT, CPT, And DBT	169
Conclusion	177

Book Four
The Power Of EMDR For C-PTSD Recovery

Introduction	181
Chapter One: Introduction To EMDR: The Basics	183
Chapter Two: Preparing For EMDR—What Women Need To Know	187
Chapter Three: Reframing And Connection—Integrating EMDR With Other Techniques	199
Chapter Four: Practical EMDR Exercises For Daily Life	209
Chapter Five: Long-Term EMDR Healing	219
Conclusion	231

Book Five
Paving A Better Life Through Resilience And Mindfulness

Introduction	235
Chapter One: Understanding Resilience—The Key To Overcoming Trauma	237
Chapter Two: Daily Habits For Emotional Health And Well-Being	247
Chapter Three: Mindfulness And Neuroplasticity—Changing The Narrative	261
Chapter Four: Creating Your Personal Resilience Action Plan	271
Chapter Five: Additional Methods For Continued Growth	281
Conclusion	291
References	293

Book One

UNDERSTANDING AND BREAKING FREE
FROM C-PTSD

Introduction

Many women carry an unspoken and invisible baggage that weighs heavily on their hearts, minds, and spirits. These are often scars from childhood trauma—the silent shadows that follow our every movement, impacting not just our inner worlds but also our most cherished relationships. This book is your guide in understanding these shadows, known in psychological terms as complex post-traumatic stress disorder (PTSD), and it is crafted specifically for you, whether you're seeking personal healing or aiming to support others through the storm.

Let's face it: Life isn't always straightforward, especially when it involves unraveling the intricacies of our past. For many women who've experienced childhood trauma or other forms of consistent traumatic experiences, there's a feeling of being trapped in a cycle of pain that seems impossible to break free from. It's like living in a loop where certain sights, sounds, or even unexpected comments can suddenly trigger a flood of overwhelming emotions. These experiences aren't isolated incidents; they often permeate across various aspects of life, affecting how we view ourselves, interact with loved ones, and navigate the world around us.

Understanding complex PTSD isn't just about labeling past experiences with clinical terms. It's a way for you to gain insights into how these experiences have shaped your life, your self-esteem, and even how you relate as a mother, friend, or partner. What does it mean to live with this kind of trauma? How does it silently influence decisions, relationships, and aspirations? Together, we will explore these questions with empathy and openness.

But enough about the weight of it all; let's shift focus to healing and empowerment. This book is about finding the light that breaks through the shadows of PTSD. Inside this book, you'll discover tools for awareness and healing, equipping you with practical strategies to transform turmoil into tranquility. Imagine having an arsenal of exercises and techniques designed to help you regain control, find peace within, and build resilience against the storms of trauma.

Breaking the cycle requires courage and commitment, and acknowledging this is the first step. Healing is not linear; it's a spiral path, where each turn brings deeper understanding and greater strength. This book is here to celebrate each victory, no matter how small, and to offer support during setbacks, knowing they too are part of the journey toward wholeness.

With heartfelt sincerity, I invite you to delve into the pages ahead. May they serve as a point of hope and a driving force for change. Yes, the process might be challenging, and yes, facing old wounds can be daunting, but the healing journey is worth every effort. Through understanding, patience, and love, you can reclaim your story, redefine your future, and emerge stronger, wiser, and more connected to the truest version of yourself. Let's get started.

Chapter One

UNDERSTANDING COMPLEX PTSD— SYMPTOMS AND CAUSES

Understanding complex PTSD involves recognizing how prolonged trauma impacts your life as a woman with undoubtedly unique experiences. While many people understand PTSD as a response to a single traumatic event like a natural disaster, complex PTSD arises from repeated exposure to situations such as childhood abuse or domestic violence.

The emotional rollercoaster that accompanies complex PTSD can be overwhelming. Those affected often struggle with emotions that feel out of proportion to their circumstances, and they may find it hard to build or maintain relationships due to lingering mistrust or fear. This struggle to connect amplifies feelings of isolation, making everyday interactions more challenging than they might appear at first glance.

In this chapter, we'll talk about the specific symptoms and causes of complex PTSD, drawing attention to how societal norms and gender-specific expectations play significant roles. Women's experiences with trauma are shaped by these factors, which influence the way symptoms manifest and how we seek help. We will also explore why conventional PTSD treatments might not be enough to address the intricacies of complex PTSD and consider more effective therapeutic approaches that can make a true difference in how you heal.

Defining Complex PTSD

Complex PTSD (sometimes abbreviated as C-PTSD) is an evolving concept in the realm of mental health that has garnered increasing attention over recent years. Unlike standard PTSD, which arises from single incidents such as a car crash or natural disaster, complex PTSD is rooted in prolonged exposure to traumatic situations. These situations can include ongoing domestic violence, childhood abuse, or captivity scenarios where escape seems impossible. This chronic trauma leads to a spectrum of symptoms distinctly different from those seen in traditional PTSD (Cleveland Clinic, 2023).

A key distinction of complex PTSD is its impact on both emotional and relational functioning. People with this condition may struggle with emotional regulation, often experiencing intense emotions that seem disproportionate to their environment. This can manifest as unprovoked anger, overwrought sadness, or seemingly inexplicable anxiety. Relationally, people with C-PTSD might find it difficult to establish and maintain healthy relationships, often feeling isolated or detached from loved ones due to persistent feelings of mistrust or fear. These emotional struggles significantly affect day-to-day interactions and exacerbate the sense of being different or damaged (Mind, 2021).

The journey with complex PTSD can be particularly challenging for women especially as societal norms and expectations play a considerable role in shaping these experiences. Women are statistically more likely to experience certain types of trauma, especially those related to interpersonal violence and abuse (Novotney, 2023). These experiences often intersect with societal pressures, such as traditional gender roles that can hinder open discussions about trauma and restrict access to support. The unique interplay between these factors compounds the already complex symptomatology of C-PTSD, which makes diagnosis and treatment even more challenging.

The multifaceted impact of complex PTSD highlights why specialized therapeutic interventions are necessary. Some strategies that can be helpful, which we will discuss in more detail throughout our time together, include:

- **Cognitive Reframing:** A strategy that helps you challenge and change negative beliefs rooted in your trauma. Recognizing these distorted thoughts means that you can begin to see yourself and the world around you through a more compassionate lens.

- **Mindfulness Practices:** Mindfulness meditation can support you in remaining grounded, helping you to manage overwhelming emotions in a healthy way. This practice enhances present-moment awareness and reduces the power of intrusive memories.
- **Building a Support Network:** Connecting with others who understand your experiences can offer validation and comfort, significantly aiding the healing process.
- **Self-Care Rituals:** Establishing routines that involve self-care can reinforce your sense of worth and belonging. Simple practices like journaling or engaging in creative activities can promote expression and reflection.

C-PTSD Checklist Self-Assessment

To help you get started with understanding whether C-PTSD is affecting you, and how it might be affecting you, you can use this self-assessment checklist. Remember that this isn't a diagnostic tool; only licensed professionals can provide medical diagnoses. However, this checklist can help deepen your understanding of yourself and where you stand today. Rank each statement below on a scale of 0–4, with 0 representing "this never impacts me," and 4 representing "this almost always impacts me."

- Section 1: Emotional Regulation
    - I feel overwhelmed by emotions I can't control.
    - I experience sudden emotional outbursts or intense anger.
    - I struggle to soothe myself when upset.
    - I often feel emotionally numb or disconnected.
- Section 2: Self-Perception
    - I feel deep shame or guilt about myself or my actions.
    - I frequently feel unworthy, unlovable, or like a failure.
    - I have a distorted self-image (i.e., seeing myself as bad, broken, or weak).
- Section 3: Interpersonal Relationships
    - I have difficulty trusting others, even those close to me.
    - I often feel detached from people or avoid forming relationships.
    - I feel overly dependent on others or have a strong fear of abandonment.
- Section 4: Hyperarousal and Re-experiencing

- I experience flashbacks, intrusive memories, or nightmares about past traumatic events.
- I feel constantly on edge, as if something bad is about to happen.
- I am easily startled or hypervigilant in certain situations.
* Section 5: Avoidance and Dissociation
  - I avoid people, places, or situations that remind me of past traumas.
  - I feel detached from reality, as though I'm watching life from the outside.
  - I struggle to remember key parts of my life or traumatic events.
* Section 6: Meaning and Beliefs
  - I feel a pervasive sense of hopelessness or despair about life.
  - I feel disconnected from a sense of purpose or meaning in life.
  - I have a hard time trusting the world or believing it is safe.

SCORING KEY

Add up your total score by combining the numbers you jotted down for each answer, then compare your score against this key:

- 0–20: Likely no significant signs of C-PTSD.
- 21–40: Mild signs; may benefit from self-help resources or speaking with a counselor.
- 41–60: Moderate signs; consider consulting a mental health professional for further evaluation.
- 61–76: Strong signs; it is highly recommended to seek professional support for possible C-PTSD.

Emotional Grounding Exercise

Learning more about C-PTSD can be overwhelming, and it doesn't help that emotional regulation is a key struggle many of us face as a result of C-PTSD. We'll cover emotional regulation techniques later on, but for now I want to share one of my favorite emotional grounding exercises with you, which you can use when you feel strong, overwhelming emotions. Here are the steps:

1. **Acknowledge five things you can see:** Look around and focus on five things in your immediate surroundings. They can be small or large, such as a book on the table, a picture on the wall, or a leaf outside the window.

2. **Acknowledge four things you can feel:** Pay attention to sensations in your body or things you can physically touch. This might be the texture of your clothing, the ground under your feet, or the warmth of a cup in your hands.
3. **Acknowledge three things you can hear:** Focus on the sounds around you. These could be the hum of a fan, the chirping of birds, or distant voices.
4. **Acknowledge two things you can smell:** Take a deep breath and identify two scents. If you can't immediately smell anything, look for something nearby with a scent, such as a candle, lotion, or the air itself.
5. **Acknowledge one thing you can taste:** Notice the current taste in your mouth. If there's none, take a sip of water, chew gum, or grab a snack to focus on this sense.

Societal Influences On Women's Trauma

Understanding the broader societal factors affecting your experiences with complex PTSD is important to discover methods for effective support and recovery. A significant barrier to understanding and supporting women's trauma experiences—even when it comes to women supporting themselves—is cultural perceptions. For example, in many cultures, there are ingrained beliefs about how we should handle stress or adversity—often suggesting resilience without acknowledging the depth or impact of our experiences. This can result in underestimating the severity of our symptoms or even blaming us for our reactions, rather than providing the necessary empathy and support. My friend Maria experienced this first-hand when her family and friends didn't understand the impact of her trauma and told her that she should "get over it." For years, this prevented her from reaching out for support.

Furthermore, traditional gender roles play a role in complicating trauma recovery. Women have historically been assigned roles focused on caregiving and emotional labor, which may deter you from seeking help or acknowledging your need for healing. These roles often imply that women should prioritize family well-being over personal wellness, which leads to a lack of self-care and delayed recovery. The burden of maintaining such expectations can exacerbate feelings of failure or inadequacy when you struggle with trauma, thus hindering the healing process.

Media portrayals also influence public understanding and often misrepresent women's responses to trauma. The media has a powerful role in shaping perceptions, and unfortunately, it frequently depicts women in a way that perpetuates damaging stereotypes. These portrayals can range from portraying women as inherently unstable to dramatizing or minimizing real trauma experiences for entertainment. Such media depictions can skew public perception, making it harder for survivors to be taken seriously and for society to cultivate empathetic responses.

Given these challenges, it becomes evident why understanding and addressing the societal factors contributing to trauma in women is so important. You deserve support, guidance, and resources as you navigate healing and recovery, because no one should have to feel alone or uncertain on this path. This book is here to provide you with a strong starting point, regardless of gender-based barriers that might feel like a roadblock at the moment.

Reflecting On Societal Influences On Trauma Recovery

*USE YOUR JOURNAL FOR THIS ACTIVITY

This activity is designed to help you explore how societal perceptions and cultural expectations may have influenced your trauma experiences, responses, and recovery journey. Set aside a quiet space and about 30 minutes for this exercise.

> **Step 1:** Write down some common cultural or societal messages you've encountered about how women "should" handle stress or adversity. These could come from family, friends, media, or even your own internalized beliefs.
>
> **Step 2:** Next, reflect on how these messages have affected you.
>
> Think about traditional gender roles and whether they've shaped your choices or behaviors. Consider roles like caregiving, emotional labor, or prioritizing others over yourself.
>
> Write about any moments when you prioritized others over your own healing. How did this affect your recovery process?
>
> With your reflections in mind, think about the barriers societal factors have created in your healing process. Write them down.
>
> Finally, write down one or two steps you could take to overcome these barriers. For example, seeking spaces where women's trauma is validated, setting boundaries around caregiving roles, or challenging internalized guilt.

Moving Forward

This chapter provided you with a look into the complicated world of complex PTSD, focusing on how it uniquely affects women like you and I. We've looked at how prolonged trauma can mess with emotions and relationships, making life feel like an uphill battle. Women face distinct challenges, often due to societal pressures and expectations. Understanding these factors can make a big difference in diagnosis and treatment because it helps tailor support to what women really need. Now, we're going to shift gears a little to discuss another factor that may have contributed to your development of C-PTSD—childhood trauma.

Chapter Two

CHILDHOOD TRAUMA AND ITS LASTING EFFECTS—A FEMININE PERSPECTIVE

Not everyone who experiences C-PTSD is someone who faced childhood trauma, but for many people with the disorder, childhood experiences play a significant role—even if you don't necessarily feel like you experienced childhood trauma.

Childhood trauma can leave a lasting impact, especially on women, shaping our lives in ways that are deeply personal yet often universal. These experiences can affect various aspects of life, and one area where this becomes particularly evident is career progression.

This chapter takes a closer look at these typically unseen challenges and offers a pathway to understanding them—all with the goal of helping you gain a deeper understanding of your own experiences as a woman with C-PTSD.

This understanding is important because you can more effectively address a concern by understanding its source, leading to healing, growth, and the ability to live authentically.

Understanding Childhood Trauma

C-PTSD resulting from childhood trauma can have lasting effects. Those of us who experienced traumatic events during our formative years—such as physical abuse, emotional neglect, sexual assault, or witnessing domestic violence—may struggle with emotional regulation, self-identity, and interpersonal relationships. The impacts of such trauma can manifest in symptoms like anxiety, depression, and feelings of worthlessness, making it challenging for us to establish trust in others or maintain healthy relationships in adulthood.

Furthermore, childhood trauma can lead to a persistent sense of shame and guilt in women. For example, my friend Rebecca faced verbal abuse during childhood, which led her to internalize the negative messages she received about herself, believing she was unworthy or unlovable. This internalized stigma hindered her ability to assert herself in personal or professional settings. Also, women who faced abandonment or neglect as a child may develop attachment issues later on in life, leading to a pattern of unhealthy relationships characterized by clinginess or detachment. These emotional scars often influence their parenting styles, perpetuating a cycle of trauma.

Letter To Your Inner Child

Understanding childhood trauma is no small task, and because of this, you don't need to understand or discover everything about your experiences at once. However, you can use this activity to help bring self-compassion to yourself as you navigate this journey by focusing on your inner child—the part of yourself wounded by traumatic experiences during adolescence.

To start, find a quiet, comfortable space where you won't be interrupted and then take a few deep breaths to center yourself. Now, think about a time in your childhood when you felt scared, hurt, or unloved. Imagine yourself as you were then. Begin your letter with "Dear [Your Name or Inner Child]," and write as if you're speaking to your younger self. Write about your experiences as a child and what hurt you—be it one incident or a pattern. Revisit the letter whenever you feel overwhelmed by self-doubt or shame, reminding yourself of the love and compassion you offered your inner child.

Impact On Career Progression

Childhood trauma has significant effects on women's career paths, as it can undermine confidence and stunt professional growth. Understanding these impacts is necessary in addressing challenges and creating successful careers.

The unique challenges women face in achieving career success can frequently be traced back to trauma-related issues. Many women who experienced trauma during childhood may engage in self-sabotage as a result of doubting their abilities and potential. This self-doubt can cause you to underestimate your capabilities and lead to choices that undercut career advancement.

For example, my friend Stacy declined leadership roles and failed to negotiate better salaries due to deep-seated fears of inadequacy stemming from her childhood. These reactions are often rooted in past traumatic experiences that distort self-perception and confidence.

Trauma also manifests in behaviors that hinder workplace relationships. Anxiety, common among trauma survivors, can lead to communication issues, making it difficult to express ideas effectively or collaborate with colleagues.

Trust becomes equally challenging; women who have endured betrayal or abuse may find it hard to trust coworkers or management, impacting team dynamics and productivity. Such outcomes not only affect individual careers but can disrupt the organizational environment as well.

Furthermore, early trauma can significantly impact job stability and satisfaction. Mental health fluctuations tied to unresolved trauma can lead to frequent career changes or inconsistent performance (*Embracing the Reality of Trauma and Its Impact in Career Development*, 2022). For example, someone might excel at work when mentally stable but struggle during particularly difficult times, resulting in unpredictable career trajectories.

In some cases, the pursuit of job fulfillment can become a coping mechanism for dealing with unresolved emotional issues from childhood, leading to a constant cycle of job dissatisfaction and change.

Activity: Exploring The Impact Of C-PTSD On Job Satisfaction And Stability

When it comes to healing from something like C-PTSD, you have more power than you think. Realizing where certain patterns stem from and taking actionable steps to address those patterns can be empowering, which is what this activity is here for. By completing this activity, you can determine where C-PTSD might be impacting your career and what you can do to change that.

PART 1: SELF-ASSESSMENT

Write down your answers to the following prompts:

- How do you feel about your current or past jobs?

  _____
  _____
  _____
  _____
  _____
  _____

- Do you notice recurring patterns, such as difficulty trusting coworkers or feeling unappreciated?

  _____
  _____
  _____
  _____
  _____
  _____

- How do you react to feedback or conflict at work?

  _____
  _____
  _____
  _____
  _____
  _____

- Do you find it challenging to maintain focus, motivation, or boundaries?

  _____
  _____
  _____
  _____
  _____

PART 2: CONNECTING THE DOTS—LINKING SYMPTOMS TO WORKPLACE EXPERIENCES

Reflect on how C-PTSD symptoms may be influencing your work life. Use the chart below to guide your thinking:

C-PTSD Symptom	Effect on Job	Example

PART 3: WHAT CAN YOU CHANGE?

Finally, write down one small step you can take to improve your work experience in each of these areas, as well as how you'll practically work toward this.

- **Trust:** How can you practice delegating or accepting help?

  _____
  _____
  _____

- **Boundaries:** What is one boundary you can establish to protect your energy?

  _____
  _____
  _____

- **Emotional regulation:** How can you respond to stress at work in a healthier way?

  _____
  _____
  _____
  _____

Gender-Based Violence And Trauma

Childhood trauma, particularly when connected to gender-based violence, can have a lasting impact on your life as a woman with C-PTSD. While each experience is unique, acknowledging the prevalence of such trauma is important, not only for individual validation but also for forming a supportive community among survivors. One in three women globally experience some form of gender-based violence, highlighting this widespread issue (World Health Organization, 2021). If you have endured such trauma, recognizing that you are not alone can be empowering as it allows you to connect with others who share similar experiences.

That said, the psychological consequences of gender-based violence experienced in childhood are enduring. Women who have been subjected to this type of trauma often face increased levels of anxiety, depression, and post-traumatic stress disorder (PTSD) in adulthood.

Societal Perceptions

Societal perceptions play a big role in complicating the healing process for women who have experienced childhood trauma due to gender-based violence. Stigma and victim-blaming attitudes can pose substantial barriers to recovery. Many women internalize these societal messages, which can exacerbate feelings of shame and guilt. Victim-blaming, in particular, often leads to self-doubt and reluctance to seek help or speak out about experiences. Overcoming these entrenched societal attitudes requires concerted efforts at both individual and community levels.

Cultural Expectations And Pressures

Cultural expectations often impose a set of standards that we as women feel pressured to meet. In turn, this can lead to feelings of inadequacy that amplify your trauma responses. These societal norms are deeply rooted in gender roles that dictate how women should behave and what we should achieve, which in turn creates an environment where deviation from these roles is met with criticism or marginalization (Lee, 2023). For women who have experienced childhood trauma, this pressure adds an additional layer of stress, as you may already be battling internalized beliefs of unworthiness or failure due to your traumatic experiences.

Family dynamics play a significant role in shaping how women cope with and understand their trauma as well. Familial pressure to conform to traditional roles can often silence those who are suffering (Ford et al., 2015). In many families, the expectation is to maintain peace by keeping issues private, which can prevent women within those families from seeking help or speaking out about their experiences. This enforced silence exacerbates feelings of inadequacy, as many of us start to blame ourselves for not fulfilling both family and societal roles in these dynamics. It's important to recognize that breaking this cycle requires immense courage and support from understanding networks that encourage openness and dialogue.

Healing: Initial Insights

Healing from childhood trauma related to gender-based violence or similar origins involves a multifaceted approach that includes education, community support, and holistic strategies. Education is a tool that can be used to inform and empower both survivors and the broader public. It helps demystify the effects of trauma and dismantle misconceptions surrounding gender-based violence. Community support is equally important because it provides a network of understanding and encouragement for survivors. Participation in support groups or survivor networks can offer insights and solidarity that create resilience and inspire hope.

Also, holistic healing strategies take into account the full spectrum of a survivor's needs, encompassing physical, emotional, spiritual, and cultural dimensions of recovery. According to Sinko et al. (2021), healing is a non-linear journey. It involves active engagement in recovery processes that integrate your trauma into your personal identity and help with moving toward future goals. Holistic approaches might include therapy, mindfulness practices, or creative expression—all tailored to meet you where you are in your healing journey.

Mapping The Path To Healing

To help you recognize the impacts of different pressures or barriers on your life, you can use this mapping activity. You'll need a piece of paper (or the space provided), something to write with (you can even use markers if you'd like to color code), and some space where you're free to think.

PART 1: CREATING YOUR MAP

1. Begin with a simple grounding exercise. Close your eyes, take three slow breaths, and silently repeat: "*I am safe. I am strong. I am allowed to heal at my own pace.*"
2. Then, write down one intention for this activity, maybe at the top of the page.
3. Draw a circle in the middle of the page and write "My Experiences" inside it.
4. Around the circle, create branches with the following categories:
    a. Emotional Impact (i.e., anxiety, shame)
    b. Societal Influence (i.e., stigma, victim-blaming)
    c. Family Expectations (i.e., pressure to stay silent)
5. Under each category, write specific examples from your life. Be honest but gentle with yourself.

PART 2: BARRIERS AND STRENGTHS

Now, fill in the chart below based on the following:

- **Barriers:** List societal, cultural, and personal obstacles to healing (i.e., stigma, internalized beliefs, lack of support).
- **Strengths:** List your personal strengths and resources that can support your healing (i.e., resilience, supportive friends, access to therapy).

Barriers	Strengths

PART 3: EXPLORING HEALING STRATEGIES

Write down at least one healing strategy you'd like to try from each category below. You can use the examples provided or come up with options of your own.

- **Physical**: Yoga, walking, or grounding techniques.
- **Emotional**: Therapy, journaling, or emotional regulation exercises.
- **Spiritual**: Meditation, prayer, or connecting with nature.
- **Community**: Joining a support group or sharing your story with trusted people.

_____
_____
_____

_____
_____
_____

Finally, set a small goal for yourself to use one or two of the above techniques:

_____
_____
_____
_____
_____
_____

Moving Forward

Exploring how childhood trauma affects your experiences, as well as the foundations of childhood trauma, can be empowering when it comes to navigating your journey. Trauma can lead to self-doubt, resulting in women second-guessing their abilities and shying away from opportunities that could advance their careers. This lack of confidence makes it hard for some women to step into leadership roles or negotiate better salaries. Furthermore, trauma can strain workplace relationships, as anxiety and trust issues may make communication and collaboration challenging. Beyond that, the circumstances that create or reinforce trauma can make it hard for us women to feel comfortable breaking free from traumatic situations, whether that comes in the form of gender norms or cultural ones.

However, it's not all doom and gloom. There are strategies for overcoming these challenges, which we'll continue to explore together during our journey in this book, and successive mini-books. With this in mind, however, we have to dig deeper into the impacts of trauma, which can help you understand your experiences and motivate you to reclaim your life.

Chapter Three

TRAUMA'S IMPACT ON RELATIONSHIPS, SELF-ESTEEM, AND MOTHERHOOD

Understanding how trauma affects your relationships, self-esteem, and motherhood is an important aspect to consider when it comes to healing from complex PTSD. Trauma can leave deep marks that alter how you interact with partners, perceive your worth, and engage in parenting. Each woman's journey through trauma is unique, but this chapter aims to offer insights into common patterns and experiences faced by many women, helping untangle the intricate web of emotions and behaviors that arise from traumatic histories.

Effects On Romantic Relationships

In navigating romantic relationships post-trauma, women often face unique challenges that can deeply impact their relational dynamics. These challenges are often rooted in trust issues that arise as a consequence of trauma, which can create significant barriers between partners. Imagine trying to build a house with walls made of glass; the structure might be beautiful but incredibly fragile. Trust operates similarly in relationships impacted by trauma. The past experiences that contribute to this fragility can lead to misunderstandings and emotional distance.

The ability to trust someone intimately is frequently compromised because trauma can instill deep-seated fears of betrayal or abandonment. You might find yourself questioning motivations and sincerity in romantic relationships, which can strain your relationships with suspicion rather than openness. This lack of trust can make partners feel alienated and, over time, result in growing separation unless addressed. It's important to acknowledge such dynamics within relationships where trauma is present. Recognizing the importance of gradually rebuilding trust through open communication and understanding is vital (Lebow, 2021).

Building Trust Activity

Trust isn't built overnight, but exercises like this one can help you get the ball rolling when it comes to healing and learning to trust again. With this activity, you can work to identify your personal barriers to trust in relationships, as well as actionable ways to communicate openly in order to enhance trust in your relationships. While this activity focuses on romantic partners, you can use it to reflect on a past relationship or even a relationship you have with a friend if you're not currently dating (which is completely fine).

PART 1: REFLECT ON TRUST BARRIERS

In the space below, reflect on the following prompts:

- What fears or doubts make it hard for me to trust my partner?
  _____
  _____
  _____

- How do these fears show up in my behavior (i.e., questioning motives, avoiding vulnerability)?
  _____
  _____
  _____

PART 2: IDENTIFY ONE TRUST-BUILDING ACTION

Think of one small way you can practice trust in your relationship or could have in a past relationship. Some ideas I came up with when I first learned about this activity—in case you need examples—included sharing a personal feeling, allowing my partner to help me with something, or expressing gratitude for my partner.

_____
_____
_____
_____
_____
_____

PART 3: PRACTICE OPEN COMMUNICATION

Finally, write a short message or rehearse what you could say to your partner (or would've said to a past one) to improve open communication within that dynamic.

_____
_____
_____
_____
_____
_____

An inability to articulate emotional needs is another challenge that amplifies relationship strain after experiencing trauma. When one partner struggles to express their emotions effectively, it can lead to pent-up frustration and conflict while deepening further emotional distance. For example, when you can't verbalize your feelings of anxiety around certain romantic gestures due to past trauma, your partner might misinterpret your silence as disinterest, leading to unnecessary arguments. This breakdown in communication creates a vicious cycle of misunderstanding that requires gentle intervention through improved dialogue and patience from both parties (Lebow, 2021).

Considering Solutions

Some specific strategies can be helpful in addressing these communication hurdles. Practice active listening and offer rephrased affirmations of your partner's statements to ensure clarity and empathy in your interactions. Also, encourage regular check-ins to discuss feelings without judgment, creating a safe space for vulnerability. For example, you can work with this simple activity to help you check in with a partner or loved one:

1. Take turns answering these two questions:
    a. "What's one thing that went well for us recently?"
    b. "What's one thing we can work on together?"
2. End the check-in by expressing appreciation:
    a. "Thank you for sharing."
    b. "I'm glad we talked."
3. Reflect in the provided space below.

_____
_____
_____
_____
_____
_____

Another aspect to consider is the recurrence of anxious or avoidant attachment styles, common in relationships affected by trauma. These attachment styles often appear due to previous experiences of inconsistency or harm, making it difficult to maintain stability in current relationships. Anxious attachment may manifest as heightened dependency or fear of being left alone, while avoidant attachment can cause withdrawal and reluctance to form deep connections. Managing these attachment styles requires effort from both partners, focusing on consistent reassurance and setting boundaries that promote mutual respect and security.

Additionally, trauma can alter perceptions of sexuality, affecting comfort levels in intimate settings. Women might experience disconnection or discomfort and experience flashbacks of past trauma in moments that should otherwise be pleasurable. For example, the intimacy required in sexual relationships might seem daunting rather than desirable, which can lead to avoidance or dissatisfaction. Addressing altered perceptions of sexuality requires patience and empathy, as well as professional guidance if needed.

Providing room for both partners to express concerns regarding intimacy without pressure can ease tensions by allowing adjustments that suit both individuals' needs.

Practicing mindfulness and incorporating consent-based practices can empower you to regain control over your sexual wellness, turning negative associations into positive experiences (Mark et al., 2023).

Challenges In Parenting And Motherhood

If you're a mother or thinking of becoming one, it's important to keep in mind how trauma can present challenges here as well. One of the most notable challenges is the transference of trauma. When mothers have experienced trauma themselves, they may inadvertently transmit their trauma responses to their children. This transference can manifest in various forms, such as replicating patterns of behavior or emotional responses. These behaviors often stem from deep-seated survival mechanisms that, while understandable, can hinder a child's emotional growth and development. Children learn by observing, and exposure to a parent's unresolved trauma can shape their own emotional understanding and coping strategies.

Another challenge many mothers face is overwhelming guilt due to perceived parenting inadequacies. Trauma survivors often carry a heavy load of self-criticism and guilt, feeling that they are failing their children. This mindset can overshadow the joys of motherhood and make it difficult for mothers to relax and enjoy their time with their children. The high standards they set for themselves can trigger a cycle where feelings of inadequacy fuel more guilt and shame.

Emotional withdrawal is another common issue stemming from trauma, which can impact attachment and bonding with children. Trauma can lead mothers to emotionally withdraw as a defense mechanism, creating a barrier between them and their children. This withdrawal can prevent meaningful bonding, which is necessary for a child's sense of security and attachment. This is another reason why trauma recovery and healing are so important for mothers or potential mothers.

To break this cycle, it can be helpful for mothers to practice self-compassion. It's important to acknowledge that parenting is challenging under any circumstances and that every mother struggles at times. Support groups and therapeutic environments can provide spaces where mothers share experiences, realize they are not alone, and receive encouragement to recognize their strengths and achievements as parents.

"One Kind Thing" Self-Compassion Activity

Whether you're a mother, prospective mother, or just a woman in need of self-compassion (and if you're here with me, then you deserve self-compassion), this activity can help add a bit of extra self-directed kindness to your life.

1. Take a deep breath and ask yourself: *What is one kind thing I can do for myself today?*
2. Pick one simple, doable act of self-compassion. Examples:
    a. Take a five-minute break to enjoy a cup of tea.
    b. Write down one thing you did well today.
3. Commit to this small act of kindness and follow through, no matter how busy your day feels.
4. At the end of the day, think about how this act made you feel, even if it was something small. Use the space below to reflect.

Body Image And Self-Esteem Issues

The impacts of trauma can manifest in how you perceive your body, potentially distorting your self-image. Women who have experienced trauma may battle with feelings of inadequacy and an inability to accept their bodies as they are. This distorted perception can significantly impact self-worth, leading to a cycle of self-deprecation and negative thoughts about one's physical appearance.

Social media plays an undeniable role in exacerbating these feelings of inadequacy. With the omnipresent exposure to idealized images and lifestyles, women recovering from trauma might feel dwarfed by unrealistic standards set by social media influencers and celebrities. These polished and often unattainable portrayals of perfection can amplify feelings of envy and reinforce the belief that their own bodies are lacking or flawed.

Furthermore, trauma can lead to deeply entrenched negative core beliefs about yourself, which are hard to shake off without deliberate effort. These beliefs can be barriers to healing and growth, trapping you in a mental loop where you continually view yourself through a negative lens. This process hinders progress toward self-acceptance and body positivity.

However, empowerment strategies can provide a pathway toward rebuilding your self-esteem and encouraging a positive body image. Mindful practices like meditation, yoga, and deep breathing allow for a reconnection with the body in a reassuring way, helping to heal the disconnection that trauma might have created. Affirmations also help, as repeating positive statements about oneself can gradually shift negative thought patterns into more constructive ones, thus promoting a healthier self-image.

Body Image Reflection Activity

This activity is here to help you reflect on any negative perceptions you may have of your body, giving you the insight you need to make positive changes. If you need space to write for any of the steps, use the space provided; however, you can also reflect internally if you prefer.

1. Find a quiet, comfortable spot where you feel safe and undisturbed. Take a few deep breaths to center yourself.
2. Write down your thoughts on these prompts:
    a. *"What messages have I received from social media about how my body should look?"*

    _____
    _____
    _____
    _____

    b. *"How do these messages make me feel about myself?"*

_____
_____
_____
_____

    c. *"What do I wish I could say to challenge these messages?"*

_____
_____
_____
_____

3. Place your hands on your chest or belly and take three slow, deep breaths. Reflect on these prompts:

    a. *"What is one thing my body does for me every day that I am grateful for?"*

    _____
    _____
    _____
    _____

    b. *"How can I show kindness to my body today?"*

    _____
    _____
    _____
    _____

4. Write down three affirmations about your body. Read these affirmations out loud or silently to yourself. Examples:

    a. *"My body is strong and resilient."*

    b. *"I honor my body for carrying me through life."*

    c. *"I release unrealistic expectations and embrace myself as I am."*

    d. _____
    _____
    _____
    _____

5. Write one small action you will take to nurture a positive connection with your body today. Examples:

    a. *"Take a mindful walk without judgment of my appearance."*

    b. *"Unfollow one social media account that makes me feel inadequate."*

C. _____
   _____
   _____
   _____

Moving Forward

In this chapter, we have delved into how trauma might be influencing your romantic relationships, parenting journey, and self-esteem. While it's not always the case that each of these areas is affected, having a strong understanding of where potential impacts lie can help you approach healing in a more knowledgeable way. When you know where the problems extend, you can address them more proactively. And, speaking of knowing those impacts, the next chapter will provide you with some excellent strategies to begin healing in practical ways.

Chapter Four

BREAKING THE CYCLE—TOOLS FOR AWARENESS AND HEALING

Breaking the cycle of trauma often begins with self-awareness and empowering healing tools. The journey to recovery can feel like an uphill battle, but it's important to remember that within each of us lies a remarkable capacity for resilience and growth. This chapter delves into ways you can harness this potential through methods designed to cultivate insight and promote healing. From reflective practices that reveal unconscious patterns to strategies aimed at building emotional resilience, the tools outlined here serve as stepping stones towards a healthier, more fulfilling life.

Journaling And Reflective Practices

Journaling is a gateway to self-awareness and healing, making it an invaluable tool as you work to break the cycle of trauma. Through the simple yet beneficial act of writing, you can navigate your inner experiences by providing a safe space to articulate emotions that might otherwise remain unvoiced. This safe haven is essential for those grappling with feelings that are challenging to express verbally.

One of the significant benefits of journaling is its ability to uncover patterns in thoughts and behaviors. When we consistently commit our experiences and reflections to paper, we begin to see connections that may not have been apparent before. For someone dealing with trauma, these patterns can reveal how past experiences influence current emotional responses and behaviors. Recognizing these patterns is the first step in understanding and eventually altering them. You can use journal prompts like these to help:

- *What recurring thoughts or feelings do I notice throughout my day?*
- *When I feel triggered, what emotions come up most often, and what do I believe causes them?*
- *Are there specific situations or people that frequently make me feel unsafe or uneasy? Why might that be?*
- *What are some patterns in how I react to stress or conflict?*
- *How do I usually cope with negative emotions? Are these coping mechanisms helpful or harmful?*
- *Are there any recurring negative beliefs I have about myself? Where might these beliefs have originated?*
- *When I think about my relationships, are there any recurring dynamics or patterns that stand out?*
- *What do I tell myself when I make a mistake? How does that internal dialogue affect me?*
- *Are there any physical sensations or body responses that consistently accompany certain emotions?*
- *When I experience joy or peace, what circumstances typically create those feelings?*
- *What are the small or subtle ways my past experiences show up in my daily life?*
- *How do I respond when someone offers me help or support? What might that response reveal?*
- *What are the common themes in my dreams, and how might they relate to my waking life?*
- *Are there any activities, places, or practices that help me feel safe and grounded? What can I learn from them?*
- *If I could identify one pattern I'd like to change, what would it be, and what small steps can I take to start shifting it?*

Furthermore, engaging with difficult emotions through journaling encourages confrontation rather than avoidance. Many people tend to shy away from painful memories or emotions, fearing the intensity of reliving them. However, by gradually exploring these emotions through writing, you can desensitize the distress associated with them and thereby ultimately reduce anxiety and stress.

Creating a gratitude journal specifically focuses on shifting attention from pain to appreciation, which can be particularly helpful during recovery. Regularly noting things you are thankful for can help cultivate a mindset that emphasizes positivity and hope. Acknowledging even small blessings can counterbalance the weight of negative experiences and memories, nurturing an optimistic outlook essential for emotional recovery. You can follow these steps to create a gratitude journal of your very own:

1. **Choose Your Journal**: Select a notebook, digital app, or journaling platform that feels comfortable and accessible for daily use. Decorate it, if you'd like, to make it personal and inviting.
2. **Set a Regular Time**: Dedicate a specific time each day for journaling, such as first thing in the morning or before bed. This consistency helps make gratitude journaling a daily habit.
3. **Start Small**: Begin by writing down 1-3 things you are grateful for each day. These don't have to be big or extraordinary—small, everyday moments count.
4. **Be Specific**: Instead of writing general statements like "*I'm grateful for my family*," try to pinpoint something specific, such as "*I'm grateful for the hug my sister gave me today.*"
5. **Reflect on Why**: Take a moment to reflect on why you are grateful for each item. For example, "*I'm grateful for the warm tea I had this morning because it helped me feel calm and comforted.*"
6. **Include Challenges**: Occasionally, write about a challenge or difficulty and reflect on any hidden lessons, growth, or support you experienced during that time. This can help reframe struggles as opportunities for resilience.
7. **Incorporate Visuals (Optional)**: Add pictures, doodles, or keepsakes that remind you of what you are grateful for. These visuals can deepen the emotional connection to your entries.
8. **Revisit Past Entries**: On days when gratitude feels hard to find, reread previous entries to remind yourself of the good moments you've experienced.

9. **Stay Flexible:** If writing daily feels overwhelming, adjust to 2-3 times a week or as needed. Focus on quality over quantity.
10. **End With an Affirmation:** Close each entry with a positive affirmation like, "*I am learning to see the good in each day,*" or "*Gratitude is helping me heal.*"

Creating Safe Environments

Creating a safe space for healing is crucial for women overcoming trauma. Feeling safe and secure can significantly impact the recovery journey, allowing you to face your vulnerabilities without fear of judgment or retribution.

A well-organized and calm physical environment at home contributes to this process. Clutter can often represent mental disorganization, potentially exacerbating stress and anxiety.

Clearing physical space can create mental space while allowing for greater focus and tranquility. Also, incorporating soothing elements like plants or calming colors can enhance well-being. These elements act as gentle reminders of peace and natural beauty, encouraging relaxation and rejuvenation.

An orderly environment can thus facilitate clarity and calmness, aiding in managing emotions more effectively. To promote emotional well-being by organizing your physical space and incorporating soothing elements that encourage relaxation and clarity, give this activity a try:

1. **Set a Goal:** Choose one small area to focus on, such as your desk, a nightstand, or a corner of a room. Write down what you want to achieve. For example, "*I want my desk to feel clear and calming so I can focus better.*"
2. **Declutter the Space:** Remove everything from the chosen area. Discard, donate, or store items that no longer serve you. Assess each item by asking:
    a. "*Does this bring me joy or peace?*"
    b. "*Is this item necessary or meaningful to me?*"

3. **Clean and Refresh:** Wipe down surfaces, dust, and clean the area. Open a window to let in fresh air or light a candle to set a calm tone.
4. Incorporate Calming Elements: Add one or more of the following:
    a. **Plants:** A small plant or flowers to bring nature indoors.
    b. **Colors:** Soft or calming tones like blues, greens, or neutrals through décor or fabrics.
    c. **Lighting:** A soft lamp or natural light source.
    d. **Textures:** A cozy blanket or cushion to create comfort.
5. Personalize the Space: Add an item that makes you feel happy or relaxed, such as a favorite book, a framed photo, or an inspiring quote.
6. **Reflect and Connect:** Sit quietly in the space you've organized and observe how it feels. Write in a journal or in the space below:
    a. *"How does this space make me feel now compared to before?"*

    _____
    _____
    _____
    _____

    b. *"What changes in my emotions or thoughts do I notice in this calm environment?"*

    _____
    _____
    _____
    _____

7. Maintain the Space: Set a reminder to tidy up the space regularly and refresh any calming elements, like watering plants or rotating meaningful items.

_____
_____
_____
_____
_____
_____
_____
_____
_____

Moving forward, it's important to not only improve your physical environment but also your emotional one because the emotional environment you experience through relationships also needs to be safe for you to heal. In any relationship, transparent communication and the setting of healthy boundaries are necessary. Clear communication allows each partner to express their needs and limitations, which in turn ensures mutual respect and understanding. Establishing boundaries helps avoid misunderstandings and reduces emotional fatigue. You can work with this activity to help you:

1. **Identify Emotional Needs**: Take a moment to reflect on your emotional needs in relationships. Write down answers to the following questions in the space provided below:

    a. *"What makes me feel emotionally safe?"*

    ------

    b. *"What do I need from others to feel supported?"*

    ------

    c. *"What boundaries would help me protect my emotional energy?"*

    ------

2. **Reflect on Current Relationships**: Think about your relationships with family, friends, or a partner. Consider:

    a. *"Are there relationships where I feel supported and respected?"*

----

    b. *"Are there relationships that drain my energy or make me feel unsafe?"*

----

3. Practice Transparent Communication: Choose one person you trust and share one of your emotional needs with them. For example:

    a. "I feel more supported when I can share how I feel without judgment. Can we work on that together?"

    b. "I need more time to myself sometimes to recharge. I hope you can understand."

4. Establish or Adjust a Boundary: Think of one boundary you want to set or reinforce in a specific relationship. Use clear and respectful language to communicate it. For example:

    a. "I need us to agree that when we're upset we take a pause rather than raising our voices."

    b. "I can't respond to texts late at night anymore—I need that time to wind down."

----

5. Check In with Yourself: Reflect on how setting a boundary or communicating your needs felt. Journal about:

    a. *"How did expressing my needs and boundaries make me feel?"*

----

    b. *"What changes, if any, did I notice in how I felt after this interaction?"*

----

6. **Create an Ongoing Plan:** Commit to reviewing your relationships regularly and adjusting boundaries or communication practices as needed.

Promoting reflection within these safe spaces is another key aspect. Intentional pauses for introspection allow you to assess your progress and recognize areas for growth. Writing down thoughts or engaging in thoughtful contemplation can help identify patterns and triggers associated with trauma. Recognizing these can pave the way for developing new coping mechanisms, gradually leading to healthier emotional responses.

Building Supportive Networks

Building a strong support network can be a lifeline as you work toward healing from trauma. Having people you trust and the right resources at your side can make all the difference in recovery. Support networks aren't just about people; they also include therapists, support groups, and online communities.

Identifying reliable support sources is essential for emotional well-being and validation of your traumatic experiences. Trusted friends or family members are important here because they offer a shoulder to lean on during tough times. They can help normalize feelings and reassure you that your reactions are understandable given what they've been through. Professional therapists, meanwhile, bring expertise to the table. Their specialized skills can guide survivors through complex emotions and coping mechanisms, ensuring they don't tackle these challenges alone (Calhoun et al., 2022).

Participating in or forming support groups is another option that provides a communal space where healing can flourish. These groups create environments where members share similar stories and struggles, leading to empathy and understanding. Support groups can be informal gatherings among peers or structured programs led by professionals. Either way, they offer a safe space to voice personal experiences and learn different strategies for managing the effects of trauma.

Moving Forward

Reflecting on the tools and strategies explored here, it's clear that overcoming the cycle of trauma is a personal journey full of discovery. And the journey doesn't end here—as we continue exploring more strategies in later mini-books, you'll find a world of tools and strategies that you can customize to your needs and appreciate as you grow.

Chapter Five

DEEPENING YOUR UNDERSTANDING OF C-PTSD

As you continue to learn about what it means to have C-PTSD, it can be helpful to understand comorbidities, daily impacts, and how to begin moving forward. This chapter centers around explaining each of these concepts, equipping you with practical strategies and exercises to assist along the way.

Comorbidities And C-PTSD

The word "comorbidity" refers to two conditions that co-exist alongside one another, usually with a high correlation between having both disorders. For example, someone with anxiety may be more likely to also develop depression and vice versa, making anxiety and depression common comorbid disorders for one another. Understanding comorbidities is important because it helps shed light on disorders that may be worsening your C-PTSD symptoms or other areas to focus on as you heal.

Disorders That Often Coincide

C-PTSD frequently overlaps with other mental health disorders. Understanding these comorbidities can help you address their interconnected impacts.

DEPRESSION

Persistent sadness, lack of energy, and feelings of hopelessness often accompany C-PTSD, which can turn into comorbid depression if C-PTSD isn't managed effectively. With this simple activity, you can track your moods to see if you're at risk of falling into patterns of depression:

1. At the end of each day, jot down your mood in a journal or tracker.
2. Use a scale from 1 to 10 and describe contributing factors. For example, "7 - Felt calm after a walk."
3. Review weekly to notice patterns or triggers.

You can use the space below to track your mood or reflect:

GENERALIZED ANXIETY DISORDER (GAD)

GAD is characterized by excessive worry or tension that's difficult to control. It's different from feeling anxious every once in a while, which is normal; GAD as a disorder affects everyday life by making anxiety excessive and difficult to manage, often seeping into many facets of life where anxiety isn't productive. When C-PTSD is added to the mix, GAD can make it more difficult to manage triggers. This activity can help you inventory anxious thoughts to begin reducing how much they affect your daily life:

1. Using the space provided or a page in your journal, write a list of common worries or intrusive thoughts.
2. Beside each one, identify if the worry is:
    a. Immediate (needs action now).
    b. Ongoing (requires longer-term management).
    c. Hypothetical (unlikely to occur).
3. Practice letting go of hypothetical worries; try to brainstorm methods to help you overcome these worries.

_____
_____
_____
_____
_____
_____
_____
_____
_____

BORDERLINE PERSONALITY DISORDER (BPD)

Emotional instability, fear of abandonment, and difficulty maintaining relationships are key aspects of BPD, but these are somewhat different from similar symptoms that arise from C-PTSD. Often, BPD can arise from trauma, which interlinks the two disorders, but BPD isn't always trauma-related. Beyond that, BPD can lead to a less stable sense of self and identity, while this isn't always the case with C-PTSD.

Key Differences

Understanding the differences between common comorbid disorders and C-PTSD is helpful because it allows you to target the individual symptoms of each disorder. While not everyone with C-PTSD experiences comorbidities, understanding the difference helps you tailor your approach to address each concern at its source for better healing. Based on what you've learned, try to identify key similarities and differences between C-PTSD and the disorders we've discussed using the chart below.

	Key Similarities to C-PTSD	Key Differences
Depression		
GAD		

BPD		

Comorbidity Questionnaire

Use the following questionnaire to explore whether you might experience comorbid disorders alongside C-PTSD. This isn't a diagnostic tool, but can help you gain greater insight into your symptoms. Answer each question honestly based on your recent experiences.

1. Do you often feel persistently sad, hopeless, or uninterested in activities you once enjoyed? (Yes/No)
2. Do you experience excessive worry or fear that is difficult to control? (Yes/No)
3. Do you frequently feel overwhelmed by intense emotions, or find it difficult to regulate your emotional responses? (Yes/No)
4. Do you struggle to maintain stable relationships due to fears of abandonment or difficulty trusting others? (Yes/No)
5. Do you notice recurring patterns of negative thoughts about yourself, such as shame or self-blame? (Yes/No)
6. Do you experience difficulties with focus, memory, or staying organized? (Yes/No)
7. Do you feel hypervigilant or constantly on edge, as if danger is always present? (Yes/No)
8. Do you often feel emotionally numb or disconnected from your surroundings or relationships? (Yes/No)

ANSWER KEY

- **Depression:** If you answered "Yes" to Q1 or Q5, you may experience depressive symptoms.

- **Generalized Anxiety Disorder (GAD):** If you answered "Yes" to Q2, Q5, or Q8, anxiety might be a significant factor.
- **Borderline Personality Disorder (BPD):** If you answered "Yes" to Q3, Q4, or Q7, emotional regulation and relational challenges may align with BPD.

Based on your answers, jot down an action plan in the space below. This might include reaching out to professionals for guidance with different disorders, doing some research on your own, or implementing practical techniques to address certain symptoms.

_____
_____
_____
_____
_____
_____
_____
_____

Daily Impacts Of C-PTSD

You might already be familiar with how C-PTSD can impact everyday life, but a lot of people fall into the trap of thinking something like, "*It's not that bad, it's not even affecting me!*" Oftentimes, this mindset stems from not truly knowing how far-reaching and even subtle some impacts of C-PTSD can be. For example, some common daily impacts of C-PTSD can include:

- Difficulty focusing or staying organized.
- Hypervigilance or feeling "on edge."
- Emotional numbness or disconnection.
- Challenges maintaining relationships.

And of course, other influences can arise as well. Fortunately, there are several tools and activities you can work with to become aware of these patterns and work to address them.

Simple Impacts Inventory

This inventory can help you reflect on the ways C-PTSD impacts you.

1. List ways you think C-PTSD affects your daily life, such as "difficulty sleeping" or "avoiding social interactions."
2. Circle the ones you notice most often.
3. Rank them by severity (1 = minor, 5 = severe).
4. Identify one impact you want to address first. Write it down and include actionable ways you can work to address this—either through options I've shared with you, options you want to explore, or options you discover later on (you can always come back to this part).

Impact Tracker

In addition, tracking the impacts of C-PTSD can help you take note of patterns and address them. In the tracker below, you can track the impacts you notice each week and compare them to the week prior to gain an overview of how your C-PTSD has changed over time, leading to more effective symptom management.

Date Range	Sleep Patterns	Emotional Patterns	Social Interactions	Focus and Energy Levels

Journaling Prompts

Journaling is another useful tool for taking note of how C-PTSD impacts your life. When you journal, you create an undeniable physical record of your experiences, making it far easier to look back on patterns you may have missed in the moment. You can journal about prompts like the following to aid with this, and the space below is yours to write in if you'd like to write in the workbook itself:

- *What was a challenging moment today? How did I handle it?*
- *What small victory can I celebrate today?*
- *How do I feel in social settings, and what do I need to feel more comfortable?*

- *What situations make me feel unsafe or on edge? How can I prepare for or avoid them?*
- *What activities or moments bring me peace? How can I incorporate more of these into my daily life?*
- *How does C-PTSD affect my ability to trust others?*
- *What triggers feelings of shame or self-blame, and how can I address those feelings?*
- *How does my body respond to stress? What physical sensations do I notice?*
- *When do I feel most connected to myself and others?*
- *What are my current coping mechanisms, and which ones feel healthy or unhealthy?*
- *What routines or structures help me feel grounded?*
- *What negative thought patterns do I notice recurring, and how can I reframe them?*
- *What boundaries do I struggle to set or maintain?*
- *What brings me joy or reminds me of my resilience?*
- *How can I practice self-compassion today?*

USE THIS SPACE AND REFLECT ON THE PROMPTS GIVEN:

_____
_____
_____
_____
_____
_____
_____
_____
_____
_____
_____
_____
_____
_____

_____
_____
_____
_____
_____
_____
_____
_____
_____
_____
_____
_____
_____
_____
_____
_____
_____

Seeing The Long-Term

It can be hard to see past your current circumstances when you're dealing with C-PTSD; however, having your eyes on the future you deserve can help you make steady progress toward the future you want, deserve, and *need,* where C-PTSD isn't the most prominent part of your day. Setting goals and reaching out for support can be valuable ways to make excellent progress toward your long-term recovery.

Setting Goals For Recovery

Goal setting is a great method to use when trying to grow in any area of life, and managing something like C-PTSD is no exception. When you set goals, you have a clear vision for what you want to achieve and can take the necessary action toward achieving it. Goals can be set in a few ways, and we'll go through some of them below.

LONG-TERM RECOVERY VISION BOARD

Vision boards are a great way to visualize what you want for your future and what it takes to get there. When you create a vision board, you put your dreams down on paper in a tangible way. This means you can always refer to your vision board when you need a reminder of why you're working so hard. To create a vision board for your recovery, collect images, quotes, and words that represent your healing goals. Arrange them on a board or digital canvas as a visual reminder of your progress. Then, reflect on the experience of crafting your vision board using the space provided below.

_____
_____
_____
_____
_____
_____
_____

GOAL-SETTING WORKSHEET

In addition, goal-setting worksheets can make a big difference in helping you plan for your goals. Give this worksheet a try:

Divide your goals into categories: emotional, physical, relational, and professional.

_____
_____
_____
_____
_____
_____

Set one short-term and one long-term goal for each category.

_____
_____
_____
_____

> Outline steps for achieving each goal.
>
> _____
> _____
> _____
> _____
> _____

Reaching Out For Support

Finally, reaching out for support can make a big difference when it comes to achieving your recovery goals. Being vulnerable enough to voice that you need help can be scary, but at the end of the day, having a strong, trusted support system can help you feel like you have someone to lean on when times get hard. Beyond that, supportive people can help us see how we can grow by offering advice or a new perspective on our circumstances. In the space below, make a list of trusted people you can reach out to, including friends, family, therapists, or support groups. Write down how you'd like to involve them in your journey, for example, "Call a friend when I feel overwhelmed."

_____
_____
_____
_____
_____

Additional Activities

Before we move on, I want to share a few more activities with you. These are all activities that really helped me in the early days of my healing journey, either by helping me understand myself or laying down some foundation for my experience with healing and growth. Take the time to work through each of the activities below.

Identifying Coping Mechanisms

Understanding how you cope with C-PTSD is key to managing symptoms. It can help you identify both helpful and unhelpful coping strategies and begin replacing those that don't serve you with healthier ones. This activity is here to help you reflect on your current coping mechanisms.

1. **Step 1**: List your current coping mechanisms when feeling overwhelmed, anxious, or sad.

   _____
   _____
   _____
   _____

2. **Step 2**: For each one, note if it is healthy (e.g., exercise, journaling, meditation) or unhealthy (e.g., substance use, avoidance).

   _____
   _____
   _____
   _____

3. **Step 3**: Identify 1–2 healthy coping mechanisms you'd like to develop or strengthen (e.g., deep breathing, progressive muscle relaxation).

   _____
   _____
   _____
   _____

4. **Step 4**: Practice these healthier mechanisms each time you notice negative feelings arising. Keep a log of when and how you use them, noting any shifts in your emotional state.

   _____
   _____
   _____
   _____
   _____

Creating A Daily Self-Care Checklist

Self-care is an important aspect of managing C-PTSD and establishing a routine can help you stay grounded and present. An activity like this one help verify that you cover various areas of self-care every day.

1. **Step 1:** Create a checklist with categories such as physical care (e.g., "Take a walk," "Eat a balanced meal"), emotional care (e.g., "Journal for 10 minutes," "Talk to a supportive friend"), and mental care (e.g., "Practice mindfulness," "Read a book").

   ----

2. **Step 2:** Set daily goals for each category and check off the items as you complete them.

   ----

3. **Step 3:** After a week, review the list and reflect on which activities felt most beneficial. Consider how you can adjust your checklist to better align with your recovery goals.

The "Take-Action" Plan

When you feel overwhelmed by the daily impacts of C-PTSD, it can help to break things down into manageable action steps. This activity encourages you to focus on small, specific actions that can ease the stress or frustration you're experiencing.

1. **Step 1:** Identify a specific situation where you currently feel overwhelmed or stuck, such as feeling like you can't focus on a task or struggling with a social situation.

_____
_____
_____
_____

2. **Step 2**: Break this situation into smaller, more manageable steps. For example, if you're struggling with focus, the first step could be "Set a timer for 10 minutes to work on one task," followed by "Take a 5-minute break," and so on.

_____
_____
_____
_____
_____

3. **Step 3**: Write down these small steps and make a plan to address them one at a time, committing to the first step as soon as possible.

_____
_____
_____
_____

4. **Step 4**: Track your progress and reflect on how completing these smaller actions contributes to the bigger goal of easing your overwhelm. Celebrate each small win!

_____
_____
_____
_____

Moving Forward

Deepening your understanding of C-PTSD and its impacts, as well as finding ways to keep yourself aware of the future you deserve, can help make your journey with recovery easier. It'll never be simple, because recovery is inherently challenging, but equipping yourself with tools like this can help you feel far more confident and less bogged down by feelings of overwhelm and uncertainty.

Conclusion

It's important to acknowledge the incredible strength it takes to embark on such a path as what you've begun here today. For every woman who has walked alongside trauma, it's important to know that your story matters and healing is possible.

Together, we've explored what complex PTSD is, how it affects different parts of your life, and some initial strategies you can use to overcome it. Reflecting on the chapters we've traversed together, it's clear that the shadows of trauma cast long, lingering effects on your life.

They seep into relationships, influence how we see ourselves, and even shape our roles as mothers if we're navigating motherhood. But these shadows don't define the entirety of who you are or can become. You hold the power to rewrite your narrative and transform pain into a foundation for resilience.

Understanding complex PTSD is more than just recognizing symptoms; it's acknowledging its intricate layers and how they intertwine with your daily life. Remember, healing doesn't follow a linear path and some days might feel like every step you take is followed by two steps backward but that's okay, because every step counts. Embracing kindness and patience towards yourself through this process is not just beneficial—it's necessary.

With this in mind, stay tuned—you're about to head into Book 2 of this mini-book series, and you'll discover the importance of emotional regulation alongside incredible techniques for honing it.

Book Two

EMOTIONAL REGULATION AND MANAGEMENT

Introduction

Welcome to the second installment of our mini-book series on healing from complex post-traumatic stress disorder (C-PTSD) designed specifically for women. If you have journeyed with me through the first book, you've already begun the needed work for understanding C-PTSD and its impact on your life.

Now, in this next step, we'll take a closer look at the emotional aspects of trauma recovery, providing you with the tools and knowledge to navigate it with greater confidence and self-compassion.

Healing from C-PTSD is not a linear path; it is a deeply personal process that requires both patience and persistence. This mini-book focuses on key aspects of emotional well-being, which form the basis of your recovery. Whether you are just beginning this journey or working to improve your existing strategies, this guide will meet you where you are and help you take the next steps toward wholeness.

Inside, we'll talk all about your emotions. This means understanding why emotional regulation is so important for trauma recovery, as well as how to identify and manage triggers stemming from C-PTSD. With practical techniques, you'll gain a deeper understanding of yourself and what you need in order to create more emotional stability in your life.

As you move through this book, remember to approach yourself with kindness. Healing from C-PTSD often brings up difficult emotions and memories, and it is okay to take things one step at a time. Celebrate every small victory, no matter how insignificant it may seem, and give yourself permission to rest when needed. Your journey is your own, and there is no right or wrong pace to follow.

Let this book serve as a gentle companion, offering guidance and support as you continue to rediscover your strength, resilience, and capacity for joy. You are not alone in this process, and every step you take brings you closer to the life you deserve.

Chapter One

THE IMPORTANCE OF EMOTIONAL REGULATION IN TRAUMA RECOVERY

Emotional regulation is key in the journey of trauma recovery. While emotions can feel overwhelming or confusing, learning to manage them effectively can be empowering and healing. This chapter dives into the fascinating role emotions play when dealing with trauma. It explores how understanding emotional reactions and responses can transform the way we approach recovery.

The Role Of Emotions In Trauma Response

Emotional regulation is a necessary component of trauma recovery because it deeply influences how trauma is processed and lived out in everyday life. When someone experiences trauma, the emotions that arise—such as anger, fear, sadness, and shame—can be intense and overwhelming (Center for Substance Abuse Treatment, 2014). If not properly managed, these emotions can significantly impact daily functioning and create additional challenges in personal relationships, work, and overall well-being.

Emotions are powerful forces that can dictate our reactions and behaviors. For example, people who have been through trauma might find themselves caught in a cycle where their emotional responses perpetuate ongoing distress. This happens when there's an inability to regulate such emotions effectively, leading to patterns of behavior like avoidance or the tendency to overreact, which ultimately hinders healing and prolongs suffering (Robinson et al., 2018).

The cycle of emotional responses often begins with specific triggers that remind us of our traumatic experiences. These triggers can be anything—from a particular smell to a place or a sound—and they bring back the emotional depth of the original trauma. Recognizing these triggers empowers you to employ proactive strategies for emotional regulation.

Developing Emotional Awareness

Developing emotional awareness is an essential tool in trauma recovery, serving as a foundation for healing. By becoming aware of our emotions, we can begin to understand how past traumas influence our current feelings and behaviors. This awareness empowers us to make informed choices that support healing and growth.

Self-Awareness Of Triggers: Trigger Tracking Journal

The first step for managing these emotional triggers is self-awareness. Keeping a journal to track emotions and noting what preceded them can be incredibly enlightening. This journal shows patterns and helps to pinpoint triggers. With this information, it becomes easier to anticipate emotional responses and mentally and emotionally prepare to handle them in healthier ways. You can use the following to guide you through setting up your trigger tracking journal:

1. **Choose Your Journal Format:** Decide whether you'd like a physical notebook, a digital journal, or an app to track your emotions and triggers. Choose what feels most comfortable and convenient for you.
2. **Create Key Sections:** Divide your journal into sections or dedicate individual pages for specific elements:
    a. **Date and Time:** Note when the event occurred.
    b. **Trigger Description:** Write down what you believe caused your emotional reaction.
    c. **Emotional Response:** Record how you felt in as much detail as possible.

d. **Physical Sensations:** Note any physical changes (i.e., tight chest, clenched jaw, sweaty palms).
   e. **Thoughts and Beliefs:** Write down the thoughts that ran through your mind during the experience.
   f. **Coping Response:** Document how you reacted or what you did to manage the situation.
   g. **Outcome:** Reflect on whether your reaction resolved the situation or intensified it.
3. **Add a Rating System:** Consider rating the intensity of your emotions on a scale from 1 to 10. This can help you identify which triggers are the most challenging and require extra attention.
4. **Reflection Prompts:** Dedicate a section for weekly reflections to summarize patterns or insights. Use prompts such as:
   a. *What patterns have I noticed?*
   b. *Are certain situations or people more likely to trigger me?*
   c. *What strategies have worked well for managing my triggers?*
5. **Review Regularly:** Set aside time at the end of each week or month to analyze your entries. This step is crucial for identifying patterns, growth, and areas that need more focus.

Validation

Another significant aspect of regulating emotions during trauma recovery is validation. In many circles, expressing emotions like sadness or fear might be stigmatized or dismissed, leaving you feeling isolated or misunderstood. Validating your own emotions means acknowledging and accepting them without judgment. With this activity, you can begin with the process of validating your emotions:

1. **Create a Safe Space:** Find a quiet and comfortable place where you can focus without interruptions. This helps you feel safe and open to exploring your emotions.
2. **Acknowledge What You are Feeling:** Take a deep breath and ask yourself:
   a. *What am I feeling right now?*
   b. *Where do I feel this emotion in my body?*

3. **Name the Emotion:** Label your emotion as specifically as possible, such as stating that you feel anxious instead of simply saying you feel upset. If you are unsure, use a list of emotions to help identify the right word.

4. **Identify the Trigger:** Reflect on what might have caused the emotion. Ask yourself:
   a. *What happened just before I felt this way?*
   b. *Is this feeling connected to a past experience or belief?*

5. **Normalize Your Experience:** Remind yourself that all emotions are natural and valid. Use statements like:
   a. *"It's okay to feel this way."*
   b. *"Anyone in my situation might feel this too."*
   c. *"This emotion is part of being human."*

6. **Practice Self-Compassion:** Treat yourself with kindness as you process your emotions. Place a hand over your heart or use affirmations such as:
   a. *"I am allowed to feel this."*
   b. *"I'm doing my best, and that's enough."*

7. **Reframe Negative Thoughts:** If judgment arises (i.e., "I shouldn't feel this way"), challenge those thoughts:
   a. Replace "should" or "shouldn't" with "I feel this way because..."
   b. Focus on the reasons behind your feelings rather than dismissing them.

8. **Write a Validation Statement:** End the activity by writing a validating statement for yourself. For example:
   a. *"I feel scared because I'm facing the unknown, and that's a normal reaction. I will take things one step at a time."*

9. **Repeat Regularly:** Make this activity a part of your emotional regulation practice. Over time, you'll become more comfortable validating and processing your emotions.

You can use the space below to write down anything you need to for this activity:

_____
_____
_____
_____
_____
_____
_____

Emotional Literacy

Emotional literacy is another component that plays an important role in this process. Understanding and labeling emotions gives you the vocabulary to articulate your feelings accurately. When we expand our emotional vocabulary, we enhance our ability to express ourselves clearly.

Emotional literacy also aids in recognizing underlying emotions, such as fear masquerading as anger. A great activity for improving your emotional literacy is as follows:

1. **Set a Timer:** Take five minutes to focus solely on this exercise.
2. **List Your Current Emotions:** Write down all the emotions you are feeling right now—no matter how small or conflicting they might seem.
3. **Sort by Intensity:** Arrange your emotions from the most intense to the least intense. For example:
    a. **High:** Overwhelmed
    b. **Medium:** Anxious
    c. **Low:** Curious
4. **Identify the Most Prominent Emotion:** Circle the emotion that feels the strongest. Take a moment to reflect on it:
    a. What caused this feeling?
    b. What does it tell you about your needs or boundaries?
5. **Take One Action:** Choose a small, actionable step to honor the prominent emotion. For instance:

a. If you feel overwhelmed, take a five-minute break.

b. If you feel curious, research or explore what's piquing your interest.

Mindfulness

Mindfulness practices also help when it comes to cultivating emotional awareness. Mindfulness involves tuning into the present moment with openness and non-judgmental acceptance (The Power of Journaling: Structured Approaches for Trauma Recovery | CPTSDfoundation.org, n.d.). Practicing mindfulness helps you learn to observe your emotions without trying to change or judge them. This practice helps break the cycle of reactive behavior by creating a space between emotion and response. For example, if I feel anxious, mindfulness allows me to acknowledge the anxiety without letting it dictate my actions.

<u>Simple Mindfulness Activities</u>

To fully harness the benefits of mindfulness, one could start by incorporating simple exercises such as focused breathing or body scan meditations into their daily routine. These exercises promote relaxation and diminish stress, making it easier to remain present and aware throughout the day. For example, give this focused breathing exercise a try:

1. **Settle In:** Find a quiet place to sit or lie down. Close your eyes or lower your gaze to minimize distractions.
2. **Start With Awareness:** Take a moment to notice how your body feels—your posture, any tension, and the rhythm of your natural breath.

3. **Engage in Focused Breathing:**
    a. Inhale deeply through your nose for a count of four.
    b. Hold your breath for a count of four.
    c. Exhale slowly through your mouth for a count of six.
    d. Repeat this pattern for 5-10 cycles.
4. **Anchor Your Attention:** If your mind wanders, gently bring your focus back to your breath. To deepen the practice, you can silently say "in" as you inhale and "out" as you exhale.
5. **Reflect:** Spend a minute noticing how your body feels now compared to when you started.

You can also work with this mini-body scan meditation to improve your engagement with mindfulness:

1. **Find a Comfortable Position:** Sit or lie down in a relaxed position where you won't be disturbed.
2. **Focus on Your Breath:** Take three deep breaths to center yourself.
3. **Scan Your Body:**
    a. Bring your attention to your toes. Notice any sensations—warmth, tension, or even numbness.
    b. Slowly move your focus upward through each part of your body: feet, legs, hips, abdomen, chest, arms, shoulders, neck, and head.
    c. As you focus on each area, consciously release any tension you feel by imagining it melting away.
4. **Stay Present:** If your mind drifts, gently guide it back to the part of your body you are scanning.
5. **Conclude With Gratitude:** Take a moment to thank your body for carrying you through the day. Then open your eyes and reorient yourself in the present.

Journaling

Journaling techniques provide a practical outlet for exploring and expressing complex emotions associated with trauma recovery. Through journaling, you create a safe space to examine your feelings without fear of judgment or repercussion.

Different journaling approaches can be utilized depending on your personal preference. Freewriting, where you jot down whatever comes to mind without censorship, encourages spontaneity and authenticity. Structured journaling, with prompts focused on specific topics, can guide users through targeted exploration of particular emotions or experiences. For example, here are some prompts that you can use if you prefer structured journaling:

- Emotional Awareness
    - *What emotion am I feeling most strongly right now?*
    - *What do I think triggered this emotion?*
    - *How does this emotion show up in my body?*
- Gratitude and Positivity
    - *What are three things I'm grateful for today?*
    - *What moment from today made me smile or feel at peace?*
    - *Who or what brought joy into my life recently, and why?*
- Exploring Challenges
    - *What is currently causing me stress or discomfort?*
    - *How have I been coping with this challenge?*
    - *What is one small step I can take to address this situation?*
- Self-Compassion
    - *What would I say to a friend who is feeling what I'm feeling?*
    - *How can I show myself kindness and understanding today?*
    - *What do I need to hear right now to feel supported?*
- Personal Growth
    - *What's one thing I've learned about myself this week?*
    - *How have I grown or changed in the last month?*
    - *What's one goal I want to work toward, and why does it matter to me?*
- Mindfulness and Presence
    - *What's one thing I noticed today that I usually overlook?*
    - *How did I stay present in the moment today?*
    - *What is something I can do tomorrow to remain more mindful?*
- Reflection and Perspective
    - *What's one past experience that shaped who I am today?*
    - *How do I want to remember this chapter of my life in the future?*
    - *What's a piece of advice I would give to my younger self?*

Guidance in using these journaling techniques includes setting aside regular time to write, selecting a comfortable and private space, and approaching the activity with curiosity rather than judgment. You should feel encouraged to explore both positive and negative emotions, understanding that each entry is a step toward healing.

Moving Forward

Throughout this chapter, we've explored why emotional regulation is so important in healing from trauma. It's clear that emotions have a powerful impact on our daily lives, especially when it comes to how we process and react to past traumas. Learning to identify and handle these emotions means that we can break free from repetitive cycles of distress and move toward healing. Recognizing triggers and developing personalized coping strategies are crucial steps in this journey. Whether it's through mindfulness, journaling, or seeking professional guidance, these practices encourage self-awareness and help us manage emotions more effectively.

Chapter Two

IDENTIFYING TRIGGERS—A WOMAN'S JOURNEY

Identifying triggers is a necessary part of understanding how past experiences can impact present emotional responses. It's often surprising to discover how certain events, words, or even places can evoke intense emotions seemingly out of nowhere. For many women, these reactions are rooted in childhood experiences that continue to shape their lives in unexpected ways. For example, my friend Alicia lived with constant anxiety in the evenings because her father would come home angry when she was a child; only after analyzing her triggers was she able to truly start leaving these feelings in the past.

In this chapter, you'll get a good look at various aspects of identifying personal triggers by exploring how our childhoods imprint on us emotionally. We'll look at practical tools like maintaining a trigger journal and using mood-tracking applications, which can help you spot patterns in your emotional responses. Sharing experiences in group settings will also be discussed as a valuable resource for gaining insight and support from others who understand what you're going through.

Linking Childhood Experiences

Early memories have a significant influence on our adult emotional responses. These experiences often influence the way we react, feel, and process situations later in life. For many women seeking healing from childhood traumas, understanding this connection becomes a vital step toward self-awareness and recovery. The emotions tied to these early memories often manifest subconsciously, triggering reactions that seem inexplicable until examined more closely.

Reflecting On Childhood Events

Reflecting on childhood events is a great place to start. Many trauma survivors find themselves triggered by seemingly unrelated adult experiences. It is important to identify specific moments in childhood that resonate as those triggering experiences. This might involve looking back at instances that caused fear, insecurity, or distress. Was there a particular event or series of events that felt overwhelming? Understandably, digging into these memories can be painful, but just know that it will empower you to reclaim your life and reduce the control these triggers wield over you.

TRIGGER JOURNAL ACTIVITY

A useful method for identifying these moments is maintaining a trigger journal. In this personal record, you can note down when you experience strong emotional reactions, such as anxiety, anger, or sadness.

Afterward, reflecting on what was happening in those moments helps trace back to potential childhood parallels. Over time, patterns begin to emerge, revealing which childhood events are echoing into adulthood. You can use the following trigger tracker to inspire your own:

Date: _____

When did the emotional reaction occur?

_____
_____
_____
_____

Briefly describe what was happening around you. Who was involved? Where were you?

_____
_____
_____
_____
_____

What emotions did you experience (i.e., anxiety, anger, sadness, frustration)?
_____
_____
_____
_____

Rate the intensity of your feelings on a scale of 1 to 10.
_____
_____
_____

Did you notice any physical changes (i.e., tight chest, clenched fists, stomach knots)?
_____
_____
_____

What was your first response (i.e., spoke sharply, withdrew, cried)?
_____
_____
_____
_____

What past experiences or memories might this reaction connect to? How does this situation remind you of something from childhood?
_____
_____
_____

What did you learn about yourself from this experience? Do you notice any recurring themes or triggers?
_____
_____
_____

What can you do next time to respond in a healthier way? Is there a coping tool or self-care practice you'd like to try?
_____
_____
_____

Recognizing Patterns

Recognizing behavioral patterns is another tool to help understand recurring triggers that stem from unresolved childhood traumas. Often, a pattern develops where particular types of interactions, words, or environments precipitate a similar emotional response—a clear sign of an underlying childhood imprint. For example, if a person notices that they feel anxious or upset every time there is criticism involved, it might relate back to a demanding parent or teacher's voice during their formative years. Awareness of such patterns allows the individual not just to predict when they may feel triggered but also provides them an opportunity to develop coping mechanisms that work specifically for these scenarios.

Spotting Patterns And Shifting Responses Activity

1. **Recall a Recent Trigger:** Think of a recent moment when you felt a strong emotional reaction (i.e., anger, anxiety, or sadness). Write it down briefly.
   _____
   _____
   _____
   _____

2. **Identify the Cause:** What happened right before you felt that way? What was said or done that triggered your feelings?
   _____
   _____
   _____
   _____

3. **Connect to the Past:** Reflect on whether this situation reminds you of something from your childhood. Ask:

    a. *Have I felt this way before in similar situations?*

    ------

    b. *Who or what from my past does this remind me of?*

    ------

4. **Notice the Pattern:** Write down if this kind of situation (i.e., being criticized, ignored, or excluded) happens repeatedly and how you typically react.

    ------

5. **Plan One Change:** Choose one thing you can do differently next time. For example:

    a. If I feel criticized, I will pause, take a deep breath, and remind myself, *"This feedback doesn't define me."*

Therapeutic Methods

Therapy offers a guided environment to deepen this exploration. Cognitive behavioral therapy (CBT) and eye movement desensitization and reprocessing (EMDR), for example, provide methods to process and reframe these memories. These techniques encourage confronting past experiences directly, allowing one to process the emotions attached to childhood events without being overwhelmed by them.

Beyond individual efforts, support groups and community organizations can play a big role. Sharing experiences in a group setting not only validates personal stories but also builds a network of shared understanding. Many women benefit from hearing others' journeys as they will often find commonalities that further illuminate their triggers and responses. You can use the following support group research worksheet to help you delve deeper into support groups accessible to you and discover what they can offer.

Research the Support Group Landscape

What type of support group are you looking for? (i.e., women's groups, trauma recovery, emotional well-being, etc.)

_____
_____
_____
_____
_____
_____

What local or online support groups are available? (i.e., Meetup, Facebook groups, local community centers, therapy groups)

_____
_____
_____
_____
_____
_____

What is the focus of these groups? (i.e., trauma healing, self-compassion, emotional support)

_____
_____
_____
_____
_____
_____

Evaluate Group Dynamics

How do participants share their stories? (i.e., open floor sharing, group therapy, structured activities)

_____
_____
_____
_____
_____
_____

What is the general tone of the group? (i.e., supportive, empowering, judgment-free)

_____
_____
_____
_____
_____
_____

Is there a facilitator or leader guiding the group? If so, what qualifications do they have?

_____
_____
_____
_____
_____
_____

Group Connection and Shared Understanding

How does the group encourage connection and shared understanding? (i.e., storytelling, mutual support, group exercises)

_____
_____
_____
_____
_____
_____

Do members actively listen to each other? How are stories received?

_____
_____
_____
_____
_____
_____

Have members shared personal stories that resonated with your experiences? Provide examples, if any.

_____
_____
_____
_____
_____
_____

Reflect on Your Needs and Goals

What are you hoping to gain from attending a support group? (i.e., validation, tools for emotional regulation, shared insights)

_____
_____
_____
_____
_____

What are your goals for being part of a community group? (i.e., to build resilience, to understand triggers, to feel heard)

_____
_____
_____
_____
_____

What do you need to feel comfortable and safe in a group setting? (i.e., confidentiality, respect, understanding)

_____
_____
_____
_____
_____
_____

Benefits of Group Participation

How do you think participating in a group will help with your emotional triggers and responses?

_____
_____
_____
_____
_____
_____
_____

Do you think group support could enhance your personal healing journey? How so?

_____
_____
_____
_____
_____
_____

Evaluate Group Fit

Does this group feel aligned with your needs? Why or why not?

_____
_____
_____
_____

_____
_____

How can you prepare for your first group session? (i.e., having a goal in mind, bringing a journal)
_____
_____
_____
_____
_____
_____

What is one thing you can bring to the group to contribute to the community? (i.e., a willingness to share, active listening)
_____
_____
_____
_____
_____
_____

Follow-Up and Reflection

After attending a group meeting, reflect on:
- What insights or lessons did you gain?
- How did hearing others' experiences impact your understanding of your own triggers?
- What steps can you take after group participation to further your personal growth?

_____
_____
_____
_____
_____

Impact Of Domestic Abuse

Experiencing domestic abuse can leave a lasting impact—influencing emotional reactions and creating triggers that complicate daily life.

Forms of Domestic Abuse

To begin, let's identify the various forms of domestic abuse that might become triggers. Understanding these can help explain why certain situations evoke strong emotional reactions. Domestic abuse isn't just physical; it encompasses emotional, psychological, and verbal forms as well.

Physical abuse often seems like the most obvious and frightening form, but the scars left by emotional and psychological abuse can be equally damaging (Lupcho, 2023).

This includes behaviors that harm self-esteem, like manipulation or constant criticism. Such experiences could trigger feelings of inadequacy or anxiety later in life. Verbal abuse, such as name-calling or threats, wears down self-worth over time, leaving behind doubts and fears that resurface unexpectedly. Recognizing these patterns is the first step toward managing them.

The emotional fallout from abuse isn't confined to the immediate aftermath. It can persist for years, affecting interpersonal relationships and overall well-being. This lingering impact underlines the importance of understanding your triggers, enabling you to manage them better.

Tools For Trigger Identification

Understanding your personal triggers involves looking within to recognize and understand the emotional responses that arise in various situations. Identifying these triggers can be an important step in healing and recovery.

Mood Tracker Tools

Mood tracking tools can be helpful by systematically logging emotions and tracing them back to specific events or contexts. These tools, which range from traditional mood diaries to modern apps, allow users to capture and review their feelings over time.

Tagging emotions to particular incidents or days means patterns can often emerge, revealing common scenarios or interactions that prompt similar emotional reactions.

Apps like iMoodJournal or Daylio are designed to help users record mood changes effortlessly, making it possible to correlate these changes with external factors such as environment and social interactions (Karimova, 2018). Alternatively, you can work with this mood tracker:

Date and Time	Mood Rating 1-10	Main Emotion	What Caused It?	Coping Tools Used, If Any

Guided Imagery Techniques

Furthermore, guided imagery techniques offer an imaginative way to address potential triggers safely. This method involves visualizing different scenarios in a controlled setting to see what emotions surface. Through visualization, you can mentally rehearse responses to known or anticipated triggers, developing a calmer approach to managing them when encountered in real life.

QUICK GUIDED IMAGERY ACTIVITY: MANAGING TRIGGERS

1. **Get Comfortable:** Sit in a quiet space, close your eyes, and take a few deep breaths to relax.
2. **Visualize the Trigger:** Imagine a situation where you typically feel triggered (i.e., criticism, conflict). Picture the details: Where are you? What's happening? What do you feel?
3. **Observe Your Emotions:** Notice your emotional response without judgment. Where do you feel it in your body?
4. **Rehearse a Calmer Response:** Visualize yourself handling the situation calmly. How do you respond? What do you say or do? Picture yourself feeling grounded and in control.
5. **Reflect:** Afterward, take a moment to check in with yourself:
    a. How did the visualization make you feel?
    b. What can you apply from this practice in real life?

Additional Guidance

It's important to approach revisiting memories with care. Reflecting on past experiences should be done in environments where you feel safe and supported, to prevent overwhelming emotions. When engaging in self-reflection or visualization, select a tranquil setting free from distractions. Use supportive tools like soft music or calming scents to maintain a sense of peace.

Moving Forward

It's clear that understanding our personal triggers is a journey worth taking. Reflecting on childhood experiences and keeping a trigger journal means that we can gain valuable insights into what shapes our emotional responses today. Recognizing patterns in interactions and environments helps us connect the dots between past and present, leading to greater self-awareness. Engaging in practices like journaling or mood tracking can further illuminate these triggers, making them less daunting to address when they arise.

Remember, this process isn't just meant for looking back—it's here to help you move forward with confidence and hope. With these tools in hand, you are equipped to navigate your own emotional landscape and continue your journey toward recovery.

Chapter Three

PRACTICAL TECHNIQUES FOR MANAGING ANXIETY AND OVERWHELM

Managing anxiety and overwhelm is central to our well-being, especially for those of us recovering from past traumas. It can often feel like an uphill battle to find peace amidst the chaos of daily stressors, but even in moments of intense unease, there are practical techniques that can help guide us back to a centered state. These methods offer you the ability to both recover from in-the-moment concerns and to cultivate resilience and self-awareness over time. Investing in these practices means you're giving yourself the tools for emotional survival and growth, and this chapter centers around these incredible techniques.

Breathing Exercises

Breathing exercises offer an accessible and effective way to manage stress and anxiety, as focusing on your breath helps invite calmness into the chaos of distressing emotions. Let's explore some techniques that can transform your response to stress. Use the lines below each activity to reflect on your experience with the activity.

Deep Belly Breathing

This technique activates your body's relaxation response, lowers heart rate and blood pressure, and reduces anxiety over time.

1. Find a quiet space where you can sit or lie down comfortably.
2. Place one hand on your chest and the other on your belly.
3. Inhale deeply through your nose, focusing on your belly rising under your hand while keeping your chest still.
4. Exhale gently through your mouth, feeling your belly lower.
5. Repeat this process slowly for 5–10 minutes, gradually increasing practice time to 20–30 minutes daily for long-term benefits.

Box Breathing

This technique provides immediate stress relief by creating a calming rhythm, promoting focus, and grounding you during moments of heightened stress.

1. Sit comfortably and close your eyes, if possible.
2. Visualize a box and follow this sequence:
    a. Inhale through your nose for a count of 4 (draw the first side of the box).
    b. Hold your breath for a count of 4 (draw the second side).
    c. Exhale slowly through your mouth for a count of 4 (draw the third side).
    d. Pause for a count of 4 (complete the box).
3. Repeat this cycle for 5 minutes or until you feel calmer.

4-7-8 Breathing

This method promotes relaxation and helps quiet the mind, making it especially effective for managing stress or falling asleep.

1. Sit or lie down comfortably, ensuring your back is straight.
2. Inhale deeply through your nose for a count of 4.
3. Hold your breath for a count of 7.
4. Exhale slowly and completely through your mouth for a count of 8.
5. Repeat the sequence for 4 cycles to start, gradually increasing to 8 cycles as you become more comfortable.

Alternate Nostril Breathing

This exercise balances brain hemispheres, reduces stress, and enhances mental clarity, fostering emotional stability.

1. Sit comfortably with your back straight and shoulders relaxed.
2. Place your right thumb on your right nostril, gently closing it.
3. Inhale deeply through your left nostril.
4. Close your left nostril with your ring finger, release your thumb, and exhale through your right nostril.
5. Inhale through your right nostril, then close it with your thumb, release your ring finger, and exhale through your left nostril.
6. Repeat this alternating pattern for 5–10 rounds, focusing on your breath and the flow of air.

Grounding Techniques

Grounding techniques also offer valuable methods for staying present and managing overwhelming emotions, essential for anyone navigating anxiety.

5-4-3-2-1 Technique

This sensory-based grounding technique redirects your focus to the present moment, helping to alleviate anxiety and stress by engaging your senses.

1. Sit comfortably and take a deep breath.
2. Identify five things you can see around you. Look closely at colors, shapes, and details.
3. Touch four things you can physically feel (i.e., the texture of your clothing, the chair you're sitting on, etc.).
4. Notice three things you can hear (i.e., distant traffic, birds chirping, or the hum of an appliance).
5. Focus on two things you can smell (i.e., your coffee, a scented candle, or fresh air).
6. Identify one thing you can taste, such as a mint, gum, or even the aftertaste in your mouth.
7. Repeat the process if needed until you feel calmer and more grounded.

Mental Anchor

This strategy uses a comforting memory, thought, or phrase to stabilize emotions and provide a sense of security during distress.

1. Close your eyes and take a few deep breaths.
2. Think of a memory, phrase, or image that brings you a sense of calm or safety (i.e., a childhood memory, a serene beach scene, or words like "I am safe").

3. Visualize or repeat this mental anchor in your mind, focusing on the feelings it evokes.
4. If you become distracted, gently bring your focus back to your chosen anchor.
5. Use this technique whenever you feel overwhelmed to regain emotional balance.

Body Scan Mindfulness Practice

This practice enhances emotional regulation by identifying and releasing physical tension linked to stress.

1. Lie down or sit in a comfortable position. Close your eyes and take a few deep breaths.
2. Start at the top of your head and slowly "scan" your body, paying attention to sensations in each area.
3. Notice any tension or discomfort in your forehead, jaw, shoulders, chest, stomach, and so on, moving gradually down to your toes.
4. When you detect tension, take a deep breath and imagine releasing it as you exhale.
5. Continue the scan until you've reached your toes, then take a moment to reflect on how your body feels.

The 1-2-3 Method

This technique helps ground you in the present moment by focusing your attention on different sensory inputs, one step at a time.

1. **Step 1:** Take a few deep breaths and settle into a comfortable position.

2. **Step 2:** Look around and identify one thing you can see. Take a moment to really focus on it, noticing its color, shape, and details.
3. **Step 3:** Then, identify two things you can feel. It could be the texture of your clothing, the chair beneath you, or the sensation of your feet on the ground.
4. **Step 4:** Finally, identify three things you can hear. Listen closely, whether it is the sound of the wind, background music, or the hum of an appliance.
5. **Reflect:** Did the step-by-step focus help you stay grounded in the present moment? How did you feel afterward?

Squeeze And Release Technique

This physical grounding exercise uses muscle tension and release to help reduce anxiety and reconnect with your body.

1. **Step 1:** Find a comfortable seated or lying position.
2. **Step 2:** Start with your hands. Squeeze your hands into fists as tightly as you can for 5 seconds.
3. **Step 3:** Release the tension and relax your hands for 5 seconds, focusing on the sensation of letting go.
4. **Step 4:** Move to your feet. Squeeze your toes tightly for 5 seconds, then release.
5. **Step 5:** Continue this process through different muscle groups in your body (e.g., legs, shoulders, jaw), focusing on the tension and release with each group.
6. **Reflect:** How did the act of tightening and releasing help you feel more connected to your body? Did it reduce any physical tension or anxiety?

Connecting With Nature

Engaging with nature reduces stress and fosters tranquility by drawing attention to the calming effects of the natural world.

1. Find a natural setting, such as a park, garden, or nearby green space.
2. Walk slowly or sit quietly, focusing on your surroundings.
3. Notice the sights (i.e., trees, flowers, sky), sounds (i.e., birds, rustling leaves), and sensations (i.e., grass under your feet, sunlight on your skin).
4. Take deep breaths, inhaling the fresh air and exhaling tension.
5. Spend at least 10 minutes connecting with nature, allowing its calming energy to ground you.

You can use the space provided below to reflect on your experience.

Incorporating these methods requires practice and patience. Each person may respond differently based on personal preferences and experiences. It's important to try various techniques to discover which works best for you. Consistent practice can lead to a better understanding of your emotional responses and how to handle them effectively.

Cognitive Distraction Methods

Cognitive distraction techniques offer a much-needed mental shift away from stress-inducing thoughts. Engaging in various activities that stimulate or soothe the mind can help you find relief and even discover new methods for creativity and personal growth. Let's explore some effective methods to help redirect focus and foster emotional well-being.

Hobbies

One way to divert attention from stressors is by participating in hobbies like painting or crafting. These activities do more than just keep your hands busy; they open doors to self-expression and creativity. Think about the sense of fulfillment you feel as you translate thoughts and emotions into colors and shapes on canvas or construct something beautiful from raw materials. It's the immersion in the task that matters—not necessarily the skill level—making it accessible to anyone willing to try. Engaging in hobbies thus serves as a therapeutic escape that improves both immediate relief and long-term satisfaction.

Puzzles and Games

Another excellent cognitive distraction comes from mind puzzles and games, such as Sudoku or crosswords. These brain-challenging activities require concentration and strategic thinking, effectively pulling your attention away from anxious thought patterns. Puzzles offer immediate distraction and improve cognitive skills over time by sharpening memory and enhancing problem-solving abilities. The benefits are twofold: while your mind busily tackles these challenges, it simultaneously cultivates resilience against stress.

Mindful Listening Exercise

When anxious thoughts become overwhelming, redirecting your attention to external sounds can help break the cycle. This exercise helps train your focus and brings you back to the present moment.

1. **Step 1:** Find a quiet space and close your eyes.
2. **Step 2:** Focus your attention on the sounds around you—distant chatter, birds chirping, or even the hum of an appliance.
3. **Step 3:** Tune into one sound at a time, paying attention to its qualities, tone, and rhythm.
4. **Step 4:** Continue listening for 5–10 minutes, bringing your focus back whenever your mind wanders.
5. **Reflect:** How did focusing on sounds impact your thoughts or feelings? Was it easier to stay present or distract yourself from stress?

Gratitude List

Creating a gratitude list is another compelling method to shift perception and build emotional resilience. This simple exercise, often done through journaling, involves jotting down positive experiences or things you're thankful for. Start each day or end it by writing three things you're grateful for. They don't have to be profound—a morning cup of coffee, a call from a friend, or a favorite song will do. Over time, this practice encourages a gradual realignment of thoughts, steering focus away from daily stressors and toward an appreciation of the positives in life.

Moving Forward

Managing stress and anxiety can feel overwhelming, but this chapter has offered you various methods to help ease that burden. We've explored breathing exercises, grounding techniques, and cognitive distractions as accessible tools you can incorporate into daily life. Each method is designed to bring calmness and clarity, whether through the steadying effects of deep belly breathing or the grounding sensations from nature walks. The goal is to build a repertoire of strategies that help you regain control and find peace, even during stressful moments.

Remember, everyone responds differently, so it's important to experiment and find what works best for you. The key is consistency and patience in practicing these techniques. As you integrate them into your routine, you'll likely notice improved emotional resilience and a greater ability to handle life's challenges. Embrace the process, and allow yourself some grace as you navigate anxiety and stress, knowing that you're equipped with practical tools for support.

Chapter Four

CREATING AN EMOTIONAL SELF-CARE TOOLBOX

Creating an emotional self-care toolbox is all about discovering what helps you feel balanced and supported. Much like piecing together a unique jigsaw puzzle, this process involves selecting practices that resonate deeply with your personal experiences and current needs. This chapter is dedicated to guiding you through creating such a personalized plan, providing insights into various strategies and methods to incorporate.

Incorporating Creativity

Creative expression is a powerful method for emotional healing, especially for those who have endured trauma. It offers you the freedom to explore emotions and experiences that may otherwise be difficult to articulate. Engaging in creative activities such as art therapy, creative writing, music, and movement can become incredible components of an emotional self-care toolbox.

Art Therapy

Art therapy uses artistic media as a form of communication that transcends beyond words. For someone dealing with deep-seated emotional scars, creating visual art can help externalize feelings and give them a tangible form. Painting, drawing, or sculpting enable you to process emotions safely and non-verbally, leading to insights and personal growth (Stuckey & Nobel, 2010). You can work with this art therapy exercise if you're interested in giving it a try:

1. **Set Up Your Space:** Choose a quiet, comfortable area and gather your materials (i.e., paper, canvas, pencils, markers, paints, or clay).
2. **Take a Moment to Reflect:** Close your eyes, take a few deep breaths, and think about an emotion or experience you'd like to express (i.e., sadness, anger, or joy).
3. **Create Without Judgment:** Begin drawing, painting, or sculpting, letting your hands move freely. Focus on the shapes, colors, or textures that feel right, without worrying about the final result.
4. **Pause and Observe:** Once finished, take a step back and look at your creation. Ask yourself:
    a. *What do the colors, shapes, or patterns represent to me?*
    b. *How does this piece make me feel?*
5. **Write About Your Art:** If you feel comfortable, jot down a few sentences about what you created and how it reflects your emotions or experiences.
6. **Reflect and Release:** Spend a few moments acknowledging the emotions you've expressed. If desired, display your artwork as a reminder of your resilience or let it symbolize letting go by storing it away or discarding it.

Creative Writing

Creative writing is another outlet that promotes emotional healing. Writing helps you delve into your thoughts and emotions in a structured manner. Writing can be a cathartic experience; it allows you to articulate trauma and gain perspective on your life stories. You can use these prompts to journal creatively:

- A place—real or imagined—where you feel completely safe and at peace. Describe its sights, sounds, smells, and how being there makes you feel.

- A letter to your younger self at a time when you faced challenges. What would you say to comfort or guide them?
- An emotion (i.e., sadness, anger, or joy) imagined as a character. Write a story about how it interacts with you in your daily life.
- A painful memory rewritten as though it had a more positive or empowering outcome. How does the story change?
- Yourself five years from now, having healed from your current struggles. Write about a day in your life and how it feels to have grown.
- A metaphorical story about a character on a journey to find a treasure that symbolizes healing. What obstacles do they overcome?
- A conversation with your trauma as if it were a person. What would you say to each other?
- A time when you overcame a difficult situation. What strengths did you discover in yourself?
- A strong emotion you've felt recently, written as a monologue from its perspective. What would it say about why it is there and what it needs?
- A magical being who grants you a single wish for your emotional well-being. What do you wish for, and how does it transform your life?

Music And Movement

Music and movement are also key practices in emotional self-care, providing different but equally valuable benefits. Music's rhythms and melodies can evoke a wide range of emotions, from joy to sorrow, offering listeners a means to connect deeply with their feelings. Playing an instrument, singing, or simply listening to music can soothe anxiety and promote relaxation. Similarly, dance and movement engage the body in the healing process, integrating physical motion with emotional expression. Movement-based therapies like dance allow clients to release tension stored in the body, creating a sense of liberation and empowerment.

1. **Choose Your Space:** Find a private, comfortable space where you can move freely without distractions.
2. **Select Your Music:** Pick a song or playlist that resonates with your current emotions. For example:
   a. Uplifting music if you need a mood boost.
   b. Soft, calming music for relaxation.
   c. Intense, rhythmic music for expressing pent-up energy or anger.
3. **Begin With Stillness:** Stand or sit quietly for a moment, close your eyes, and take a few deep breaths. Tune in to your body and notice any tension or emotions you are carrying.
4. **Let Your Body Respond:** As the music plays, allow your body to move naturally. Start small—swaying, tapping your feet, or nodding your head—and let the movements grow as you feel more comfortable. Don't worry about how it looks; focus on how it feels.
5. **Engage Fully:** If you're feeling joyful, let the music inspire energetic, free-flowing movements. If you're working through sadness or frustration, move slowly and deliberately, allowing those emotions to flow through your body. Consider singing or humming along to deepen your connection with the music.
6. **Reflect:** After the song or playlist ends, sit quietly and reflect on how you feel. Did the movement help you release any tension or emotions? What insights, if any, did you gain?
7. **Journaling:** Write a few sentences or phrases about your experience. What emotions came up? How did the music and movement impact your mood?

Setting Healthy Boundaries

Establishing boundaries is an important part of maintaining emotional well-being and personal growth. When you set clear limits, you can protect yourself from emotional burnout, manage your energy effectively, and cultivate healthier relationships. Let's dive into how boundaries work and why they are so vital.

Identifying Personal Limits

The first step in establishing effective boundaries is identifying your personal limits. Understanding your own needs and recognizing your limits can help prevent burnout and ensure you have the necessary resources to face daily challenges. When you know where your boundaries exist, it can be far easier to navigate relationships without feeling overwhelmed or taken advantage of. To identify personal limits, you can work with this activity:

1. **Reflect on Discomfort:** Think of recent situations where you felt uncomfortable, stressed, or drained. Note what caused those feelings.
2. **Spot Patterns:** Identify recurring scenarios or interactions that consistently make you uncomfortable.
3. **Create a "No" List:** Write down situations or requests you will start saying "no" to, like overcommitting or taking on tasks you don't value.
4. **Practice Saying "No":** Come up with respectful responses, like "I can't commit to this right now, but thank you for asking."
5. **Apply and Reflect:** Track situations where you set boundaries over the next week and note how it felt. Adjust as needed to protect your peace.

Effective Communication

Another key aspect of boundary setting is communicating them effectively. The way you express your limits and needs can significantly impact how they're respected by others. Clear communication minimizes misunderstandings and ensures that your boundaries are recognized and adhered to within your relationships. You can use this activity to become familiar with something known as "I" statements, which help communication be more respectful and authentic:

1. **Practice Using "I" Statements:** Rewrite the following accusatory statements into "I" statements:

    a. "You never listen to me!"

    _____
    _____
    _____
    _____
    _____

    b. "You are always interrupting my work."

    _____
    _____
    _____
    _____

    c. "You make me feel ignored."

    _____
    _____
    _____
    _____
    _____

2. **Reflect on a Personal Boundary:** Think of a situation where you need to set a boundary. Write down:

    a. The boundary you want to express.

    _____
    _____
    _____
    _____

    b. How you will use an "I" statement to communicate it.

----

3. **Plan for Boundary Crossings:** Write down how you will respond if someone crosses your boundary.

   ----

4. **Apply and Reflect:** Over the next week, practice using "I" statements in conversations. Reflect on the results:

   a. Did it reduce conflict?

   ----

   b. How did you feel after expressing yourself?

Consistent Enforcement

Once boundaries are established, consistently enforcing them is crucial. Consistency reinforces your self-worth and clarifies expectations in relationships. When you maintain your boundaries, you reduce confusion and promote mutual respect. Inconsistently applied boundaries might give mixed signals, leading to further misunderstandings and possibly eroding trust.

Flexibility

Boundaries are not rigid—they may evolve over time and need revisiting as circumstances change. Life events, new relationships, or shifts in priorities can prompt the need to adjust your limits. Regular reflection allows you to evaluate whether your current boundaries still align with your values and meet your needs. Practicing adaptability ensures that your emotional self-care toolbox remains effective and relevant to your life's current pace.

Mindful Relaxation Practices

Mindful relaxation techniques also belong in your emotional self-care toolbox, no matter if you're navigating challenging emotions or striving for a more balanced state of mind. These practices go beyond simple stress relief; they leave you with a strong sense of presence and inner peace.

Meditation

Meditation can be a gentle guide to reconnecting with yourself. It helps quiet the chaos within and invites a calming rhythm into your life. The practice creates a space where you can observe thoughts without judgment, which also allows for a deeper connection to your true self. If you'd like to try a short meditation now, you can use the following steps:

1. Sit or lie down in a quiet space. Close your eyes and take a deep breath in, then slowly exhale.
2. Bring your attention to your breath, noticing the rise and fall of your chest or abdomen. Don't try to control it, just observe.
3. As thoughts arise, simply notice them without judgment. Imagine them as clouds passing by—acknowledge them and then let them drift away.
4. With each breath, feel a wave of relaxation washing over you. Allow this calmness to spread through your body, from your head to your toes.
5. For the next few minutes, simply be present with your breath, your body, and the space around you. There's no need to change anything, just observe.
6. Slowly bring your awareness back to the room. Take a deep breath and gently open your eyes. Notice how you feel now compared to when you began.

Breathing Techniques

Next, consider incorporating breathing techniques into your routine. Breathwork is a simple yet powerful way to activate the body's natural relaxation response. When you're feeling anxious, focusing on controlled breathing can help manage that anxiety and improve concentration. We discussed many different breathing techniques in the previous chapter, which are helpful to revisit for mindfulness.

Creating Your Self-Care Plan

The goal of this activity is to build a personalized emotional self-care plan that incorporates practices you enjoy and find beneficial. Selecting and combining different strategies helps you create a toolbox to manage stress and emotional pain, promoting healing.

Step 1: Identify Your Emotional Needs

Take a moment to reflect on your current emotional state. What are you feeling today? Are there specific emotions you wish to address or work through (i.e., stress, sadness, frustration, joy)?

- What emotions are most challenging for you right now?
- What practices have helped you in the past during tough emotional times?

Write down your responses.

_____
_____
_____
_____
_____
_____

Step 2: Select Your Emotional Self-Care Practices

Below are a few emotional self-care practices to consider. Choose the ones that resonate with you most, or combine a few from different categories.

- Creative Practices:
    - Art Therapy: Express your emotions through drawing, painting, or sculpting. You can create a piece that represents how you are feeling or explore abstract forms.
    - Creative Writing: Journal your emotions or write short stories using the prompts provided in this chapter.
    - Music & Movement: Choose music that fits your mood or move your body to release tension.
- Relaxation Practices:
    - Meditation: Practice daily meditation to quiet the mind and center yourself.
    - Breathing Techniques: Incorporate deep belly breathing, box breathing, or 4-7-8 breathing into your routine.
- Boundary Practices:
    - Setting Boundaries: Reflect on your personal limits and identify situations where you need to say "no" to protect your emotional well-being.
    - Effective Communication: Practice using "I" statements to express your needs in a calm and assertive manner.
- Nature Connection:
    - Engaging With Nature: Spend time outside, walk in a park, or sit near a tree to restore balance.

Step 3: Create Your Self-Care Plan

Using the practices you've selected, create a plan to incorporate them into your daily or weekly routine. Consider your schedule and how much time you can realistically dedicate to self-care.

- Daily Practices: What time of day works best for these practices? How often will you engage in them (i.e., every morning, once a day)?
- Weekly Practices: Set aside a specific time each week for creative expression or movement. What days of the week will you engage in these practices?

Step 4: Track Your Progress

Over the next week, practice using the strategies you've included in your self-care plan. Keep a journal or log to track how each practice makes you feel.

- How do you feel before and after each practice?
- Are there any emotions or thoughts that arise during these activities?
- Which practices feel the most effective for you?

Feel free to use the space provided below to track your progress.

Step 5: Reflect And Adjust

At the end of the week, reflect on your experience. Do you feel more grounded or connected to your emotions? Adjust your plan as needed and use the space provided to answer these questions if you like.

- What practices were most helpful?
- What would you like to incorporate more of?
- What needs to be adjusted to fit your lifestyle?

Moving Forward

Remember, emotional self-care is all about finding what works best for you and your journey. In this chapter, we explored the power of creative expression through art, writing, music, and movement as tools to heal and understand emotions. Each form of creativity offers a unique way to connect with your feelings and experiences.

As you create your own emotional self-care plan, consider how these creative practices fit into your life. It's important to choose activities that resonate with you personally. Your plan should reflect your preferences and needs, allowing you to express yourself in ways that feel natural and fulfilling. This means giving yourself permission to say "no" to things that don't serve your well-being and making space for those that do. Ultimately, this personalized approach empowers you to heal at your own pace, using creativity as a guide to rediscovering strength and resilience.

Chapter Five

RECEIVING EMOTIONAL SUPPORT FROM OTHERS

As you navigate the world of emotional management as someone with C-PTSD, it can be hard to reach out for support. However, receiving support from others is an important part of healing as social networks help us thrive in different parts of our lives. With someone you can trust by your side, you have someone to share experiences with, receive advice from, and ultimately gain a rewarding relationship with. It's these connections that help you break free from relationship patterns that connect with C-PTSD. In this chapter, you'll discover techniques and strategies that will help you become more comfortable with receiving support from others while still maintaining a healthy balance of independence.

Asking Others For Support

Asking others for support can be scary. It requires a level of vulnerability that can be hard to extend following traumatic experiences, but being able to extend vulnerability and trust to others is a part of healing from those experiences. Asking others for support means that you don't have to brave the experience of C-PTSD recovery alone, that you can receive advice and guidance from people with similar experiences, and that you can form a network of loving people who uplift you and who you can uplift in return.

Building Trust

Part of asking others for support means re-learning how to trust. For some people with C-PTSD, trust can be challenging—I personally experienced this when I found myself unable to trust loved ones after my trauma, even if they gave me no reason to be distrustful. While simple activities won't magically fix your trust overnight, working with activities like the following can help you begin to rebuild that trust.

TRUST TIMELINE

Rebuilding trust often involves recognizing its foundation and reflecting on its loss. This activity helps you identify moments when trust was built or broken, providing insight into your feelings.

1. On a piece of paper, draw a horizontal line.
2. Mark key life events above the line where trust was built (e.g., "My best friend supported me in hard times," or "I felt safe with my grandmother").
3. Below the line, note events where trust was broken (e.g., "I confided in someone who betrayed me," or "I experienced a harmful relationship").
4. For each positive moment, write about what made you feel safe and secure. For each challenging moment, describe how it affected your ability to trust others or yourself.
5. Look for patterns. For example, do you trust people who show consistent actions? Are broken trust events tied to specific types of behavior?
6. Circle one positive event and ask yourself, "How can I recreate this type of trust in a current relationship?" You can write your answer below.

_____
_____
_____
_____
_____
_____

THE TRUST JAR

This activity is a visual way to rebuild trust in relationships and recognize small, trustworthy actions over time.

Supplies:
- A jar or container.
- Small objects (e.g., marbles, buttons, or pebbles).

Instructions:
1. Write the name of a person you want to work on trusting more (e.g., "Mom," "My partner," or even "Myself") and place it on the jar.
2. Each time the person (or you) does something that feels trustworthy, add one object to the jar. For example:
    a. "They kept their promise to meet me on time."
    b. "I set a boundary, and they respected it."
    c. "I followed through on a commitment to myself."
3. At the end of each week, look at the jar and write about what contributed to the trust you are building.
4. Once the jar is full, celebrate by acknowledging how trust has grown and consider a small reward that symbolizes your progress (e.g., a new journal, a self-care activity, or sharing gratitude with the person).

Reaching Out

Once you feel ready enough to reach out for support, how can you actually go about reaching out? These activities can be a big help!

SUPPORT CIRCLE MAPPING

1. On a blank piece of paper, draw a large circle divided into three rings (like a target). Label the center ring "Closest Support," the middle ring "Trusted Support," and the outer ring "Occasional Support."
2. Think about the people in your life and where they might fit:
    a. **Closest Support**: People you trust most and can be vulnerable with (e.g., a best friend, therapist, or partner).
    b. **Trusted Support**: People you trust but don't go to for everything (e.g., extended family, coworkers, or acquaintances).
    c. **Occasional Support**: People you might reach out to for specific needs (e.g., a neighbor or a teacher).
3. Next to each person's name, write what type of support they could offer, such as:

a. Emotional (listening, understanding).

   b. Practical (help with errands or advice).

   c. Professional (therapy, medical guidance).

4. Choose one person to reach out to and draft a short message or conversation starter, like:

   a. "I've been feeling overwhelmed lately, and I could use someone to talk to. Are you available?"

THE SUPPORT SCRIPT BUILDER

When you are nervous about reaching out, having a script can ease the pressure. This activity helps you create a personalized message or conversation opener.

1. Ask yourself what you want from the interaction:

   a. Do you need someone to listen?

   b. Are you asking for advice?

   c. Do you need help with a task?

2. Use this template to create your script:

   a. **Greeting:** "Hi [Name], I hope you are doing well."

   b. **State Your Need:** "I've been going through [brief description of what's been difficult], and I feel like I could use some support."

   c. **Ask for Specific Help:** "Would you be able to [listen/talk/help me with...]?"

   d. **Closing:** "I really appreciate you taking the time to [whatever they'd be doing]. Thank you so much."

   e. **Example:**

      i. "Hi Sarah, I hope you are doing well. I've been feeling really stressed lately and could use someone to talk to. Would you be able to grab a coffee and chat sometime this week? I'd really appreciate it."

3. Say your script out loud to yourself or write it in a message format. Adjust it as needed to feel authentic and comfortable.

4. Send your message or have the conversation. Afterward, reflect on how it went and celebrate your bravery in reaching out.

Balancing Support With Independence

Reaching out for support is always a good thing, but it's important to balance that support with independence. Without careful consideration, it can become easy to over-rely on those in your support network, which can stunt your growth and put a strain on relationships. Besides, independence is important to your recovery! Recovering from C-PTSD and gaining a healthy level of dependence means that you can rely on yourself to tell you what your values are, what you believe, and what you're worth, preventing toxic people from regaining control in your life.

Activities for Healthy Independence

A few different activities can be helpful as you learn to cultivate healthy independence in recovery.

VALUE DISCOVERY JOURNAL

1. In your journal or the space below, list five values that are most important to you (e.g., honesty, kindness, creativity). For each value, write why it is important to you and how it shapes your decisions.
2. Write down three beliefs about yourself that you hold (e.g., "I am capable," "I deserve love and respect"). Reflect on how these beliefs influence your choices and behaviors.
3. Turn your values and beliefs into affirmations. For example:
    a. **Value:** "Honesty is important to me."
    b. **Affirmation:** "I value honesty and live my life with integrity."
4. Read your affirmations every morning and reflect on how you embody your values throughout the day.

<u>Problem-Solving Solo</u>

This activity helps you build confidence in solving challenges independently.

1. Write down a problem you are currently facing (e.g., managing your schedule, setting boundaries).
2. Without asking for help, list as many solutions as you can. Be creative and don't worry if they seem imperfect.
3. Choose one solution and break it into small, actionable steps. Write a plan and commit to trying it out.
4. After implementing your solution, reflect on what worked, what didn't, and how you felt taking charge.

Activity for Understanding Over-Reliance

It can be challenging to understand when you may be verging on over-relying on others. With activities, you can strengthen your understanding of over-reliance and how to balance it alongside independence. This activity helps you evaluate whether you are relying too much on others or maintaining a healthy balance. Start by filling out this chart over the course of a week:

What I Needed Help With	Who I Asked for Help	Could I Have Done It Alone?

At the end of the week, review your chart. Look for patterns, such as consistently seeking help for tasks you might be capable of handling independently. Commit to trying one task independently next week and reflect on how it felt.

Keep in mind, however, that there is no problem with asking for help with a task you could've done alone if it helps you feel supported and cared for. A concern only comes into play when you rely too much on others for tasks you can handle yourself—and potentially *should* handle yourself as a part of your recovery.

Moving Forward

Finding support while balancing healthy levels of independence is a crucial part of your journey. With a strong support network, the ability to trust in others, and the ability to feel confident while independent, you can make managing C-PTSD less of a struggle and more about moving forward and growing.

Conclusion

As you close this section of the book, take a moment to recognize how far you've come in understanding and managing the complexities of emotional regulation. This journey isn't about perfection—it is about progress, compassion for yourself, and small, meaningful steps toward healing.

Through this book, you've explored the incredible power of emotional regulation and the ways it can help you reclaim control over your mind and body. You've learned to:

- Identify and understand your unique triggers, empowering you to anticipate and navigate challenging situations.
- Manage anxiety and overwhelm with practical techniques that ground and center you in moments of distress.
- Build your own emotional self-care toolbox—a collection of personalized strategies to nurture your mental and emotional well-being.
- Take the courageous step of asking for support and deepening your connections with trusted people in your life.

These tools are here to create space for joy, growth, and connection, even in the face of the challenges that C-PTSD can bring. As you move forward, remember that healing is a journey, not a linear path. There will be ups and downs, but in all of it, you are building a basis of resilience, self-awareness, and self-compassion in your life.

Keep using the tools you've discovered here. Continue to grow your emotional self-care toolbox, fine-tune your techniques, and lean on your support system when you need it. Most importantly, remind yourself often of your incredible courage. Every step you take toward healing is a victory worth celebrating. You've already proven how strong and capable you are. Keep going, one step at a time. You've got this.

Book Three

MANAGING C-PTSD THROUGH PROFESSIONAL THERAPEUTIC TECHNIQUES

Introduction

Healing from complex post-traumatic stress disorder (C-PTSD) is a deeply personal journey that requires patience, compassion, and a willingness to engage with the painful past in order to build a healthier future.

For many women, such as you and I, the path to healing is not linear and may involve unlearning patterns of self-doubt, fear, and isolation that have taken root over years of trauma. However, the healing process also offers an opportunity to rediscover your strength, reclaim your personal power, and develop new ways of coping with life's challenges.

This mini-book is designed to guide you through key therapeutic approaches, beginning with cognitive processing therapy (CPT), a proven method for reshaping the ways in which we perceive and respond to trauma. Exploring negative core beliefs and learning how to reframe them is something else we'll touch on, which will help you begin to unlock the possibility of healing from wounds that may have been buried for years.

In addition to CPT, this guide will walk you through other therapeutic practices, incorporating a holistic approach that addresses the mind, body, and spirit in a compassionate and integrated way.

Each chapter is designed to offer both practical tools and insightful reflections to support you as you navigate the complexities of healing from C-PTSD as a woman. It is my hope that you find both solace and strength in these pages as you take the next steps toward reclaiming your life, your peace, and your sense of self.

Chapter One

INTRODUCTION TO COGNITIVE PROCESSING THERAPY

Cognitive processing therapy, or CPT for short, is a tool that's changing the way we approach trauma recovery. Feelings of self-blame, anxiety, or depression are all areas where CPT can give you the tools you need to face these challenges head-on.

In this chapter, we're going to get into the nuts and bolts of how CPT works its magic. We'll talk about concepts like cognitive restructuring, which helps break those stubborn negative thought patterns, and narrative reconstruction, which allows you to rewrite your trauma stories in ways that promote healing and empowerment.

You'll also learn about the importance of building a strong therapeutic alliance—a partnership between therapist and client that's important for tackling tough topics together. This chapter lays out everything you need to understand why CPT is such a game-changer.

Fundamental Principles Of CPT

Cognitive processing therapy (CPT) is designed to help people struggling with the impact of traumatic experiences by focusing on how they think and feel about their trauma.

This approach offers a structured way to tackle trauma by addressing negative thoughts and beliefs. Through its core components, CPT empowers us to process our trauma more healthily and promotes healing and recovery.

Cognitive Restructuring

A core aspect of CPT is cognitive restructuring, which helps you identify and challenge negative thoughts associated with your trauma. Negative thoughts about oneself or the world can become ingrained after a traumatic event, which can in turn lead to feelings of helplessness, anxiety, or depression. Cognitive restructuring provides you with tools to question these thoughts, ultimately improving self-awareness. For example, someone might believe they are responsible for a traumatic event but through cognitive restructuring, they learn to consider alternative explanations and assess evidence more objectively.

SIMPLE RESTRUCTURING EXERCISE

To effectively implement cognitive restructuring, it is important to create an atmosphere where you feel comfortable challenging your thoughts. This involves actively engaging in exercises that question the validity of your negative beliefs. Encouragingly, this process improves day-to-day coping mechanisms and equips you with skills to handle future challenges. For example, you can give this exercise a try:

1. **Identify the Negative Thought:** Write down a distressing thought that has been bothering you.
2. **Assess the Evidence:**
    a. What evidence supports this thought?
    b. What evidence contradicts it?
3. **Consider Alternative Perspectives:** Imagine a friend telling you this thought—how would you respond to them?
4. **Reframe the Thought:** Rewrite the thought in a more balanced, compassionate way.
5. **Notice the Emotional Shift:** After reframing, check in with how you feel. Do you notice any reduction in distress?

_____
_____
_____
_____
_____
_____

Narrative Reconstruction

Narrative reconstruction is another important component of CPT that can help you explore and redefine your trauma narratives. Trauma can distort personal stories and impact how you view your life events or personal identity. In narrative reconstruction, you are encouraged to recount your trauma in detail. This helps you seek meaning in what happened and validate your emotions. You can work with this narrative reconstruction exercise to try the process for yourself:

1. **Set a Safe Environment:** Find a quiet, comfortable space where you feel secure. Have a comforting object nearby (e.g., a soft blanket, a calming scent, or a warm drink).
2. **Begin by Writing Your Story:** Describe the traumatic event in detail, as if you were telling a story. Focus on what happened, your emotions at the time, and how it has impacted you. Write without judgment—just let the words flow.
3. **Identify the Distortions:** Review your story and highlight any negative core beliefs that surface (e.g., *"It was my fault," "I am weak," "I will never be safe"*). Ask yourself: Are these beliefs based on fact or fear?
4. **Reframe With Compassion:** Rewrite the story from a compassionate, empowered perspective. Acknowledge the pain but also recognize your strength.
    a. Example: Instead of "I was powerless," reframe it as "I survived something difficult, and that shows my resilience."
5. **Find Meaning in Your Story:** Reflect on what you've learned about yourself. What strengths have you developed from your experience? How can this new perspective help you move forward?
6. **End With Self-Validation:** Write a statement affirming your growth.
    a. Example: *"My trauma does not define me. I am healing, and I deserve peace."*

Therapeutic Alliance

The success of CPT hinges on therapeutic alliance, which emphasizes a collaborative relationship between therapist and client. A strong therapeutic alliance builds trust and facilitates open communication, which is necessary for digging into difficult topics. When clients see therapists as allies rather than authority figures, they are more likely to engage honestly in the therapy process. This partnership enables clients to feel supported, heard, and understood, making it easier to confront painful memories and emotions. If you're considering professional guidance, the following exercise can help you approach therapy as more of an alliance for enhanced success:

1. **Clarify Your Therapy Goals:** Before your next session (or if you are considering therapy), write down what you hope to gain from therapy.
    a. Example: "I want to understand and challenge my negative core beliefs."
2. **Identify Your Communication Style:** Reflect on how you typically express emotions and concerns.
    a. Example: Do you feel comfortable speaking openly, or do you tend to hold back?
3. **Express Your Needs to Your Therapist:** At the beginning of a session, communicate what you need from your therapist to feel safe and supported.
    a. Example: "I need reassurance that I won't be judged for my feelings."
4. **Practice Collaborative Language:** Instead of seeing the therapist as an authority figure, view them as a partner. Try using phrases like:
    a. "Can we explore this thought together?"
    b. "I'd like to understand this from another perspective."

5. **Give and Receive Feedback:** If something in therapy isn't working, express it.
   a. Example: "I feel like we focus a lot on my past, but I'd like more coping strategies for the present."
6. **Reflect on the Relationship:** After a session, journal about how you felt:
   a. Did you feel heard and validated?
   b. Was there anything you wish you had said or asked?
   c. Do you feel like you and your therapist are working as a team?

Goal Setting

Furthermore, goal-setting is a big part of CPT. It supports progress measurement and motivation by aligning therapy or therapeutic methods with your individual aspirations. Setting clear goals helps you focus on what you wish to achieve through therapy, whether it is reducing anxiety, overcoming nightmares, or regaining confidence. Take some time to set some short- and long-term goals for CPT, if you're interested, with the worksheet below.

How It Differs From Other Therapies

Unlike other therapeutic modalities, CPT places significant emphasis on addressing and changing cognitive distortions, making it particularly effective in altering the negative thought patterns associated with trauma.

One of the unique features of CPT is its focus on cognition. Trauma can severely impact our thinking patterns, which can then lead to distorted beliefs and assumptions about yourself and the world. These cognitive distortions often include feelings of self-blame, denial, and overgeneralization, which can perpetuate emotional distress and hinder recovery.

Socratic Questioning

CPT actively engages you in challenging these distorted beliefs through techniques like Socratic questioning and structured worksheets. Here's a simple Socratic questioning exercise you can try:

1. **Identify a Distressing Thought:** Write down a negative or self-critical thought that frequently comes up.
    a. Example: "*I am unworthy of love because of my past.*"
2. **Examine the Evidence:**
    a. Ask yourself: What evidence supports this thought?
    b. Then ask: What evidence contradicts it?
    c. Example: "*I have friends and family who care about me. My past does not define my worth.*"
3. **Consider Alternative Perspectives:** Imagine someone else in your situation—what would you say to them?
    a. Example: "*I would never tell a friend they are unworthy of love because of their past. Why do I believe that about myself?*"
4. **Assess the Impact of the Thought:** How does believing this thought make you feel? Does it help or hinder your healing process?
    a. Example: "*This thought makes me feel hopeless and isolated. It prevents me from building meaningful connections.*"
5. **Reframe with a Balanced Thought:** Rewrite the thought in a more objective and compassionate way.
    a. Example: "*My past experiences do not determine my worth. I am capable of growth, love, and connection.*"
6. **Notice Emotional Shifts:** After reframing, check in with how you feel. Do you notice a sense of relief or empowerment?

The structured timeline within CPT is another distinctive aspect. For many people new to therapy, the uncertainty and open-ended nature of traditional therapeutic approaches can heighten anxiety. CPT alleviates this concern by providing a clear and consistent framework. The therapy typically unfolds over a set number of sessions, each with specific objectives and exercises. This predictability helps clients know what to expect.

Moving Forward

Together, we've explored the ins and outs of cognitive processing therapy (CPT) and how it can be a game-changer for those working through trauma. We've dug into the importance of challenging those pesky negative thoughts that tend to hang around after a traumatic event. Applying cognitive restructuring helps you learn to swap out these thoughts with more balanced ones, which makes it easier to regain control over your emotions and reactions. Narrative reconstruction adds another layer by allowing you to reframe your personal stories in immensely positive ways.

We also touched on how crucial a strong therapeutic alliance is in making CPT successful. Building trust and open communication between therapist and client means that therapy becomes a safe space to tackle difficult emotions and thoughts. Setting goals throughout the process keeps everything on track, providing direction and boosting motivation as small victories are celebrated along the way.

Chapter Two

IDENTIFYING NEGATIVE CORE BELIEFS

Recognizing negative core beliefs is a necessary step in the journey to understanding ourselves better. These beliefs, often buried deep within us, shape how we perceive our worth and capability. They can silently influence every decision we make and interaction we have. Realizing their hold over our thoughts and actions can be eye-opening yet daunting. However, confronting these beliefs opens up the possibility for growth, allowing you to reclaim control over your life.

In this chapter, we'll explore the roots of these negative core beliefs, including where they come from and how they take hold. You'll read about influences ranging from family dynamics to societal norms, all contributing to the experiences and stories we carry around with us. The discussion will extend to how traumatic experiences and personal relationships can reinforce or challenge these beliefs. Through a blend of insights and practical guidance, this chapter seeks to equip you with tools to navigate and ultimately transform those entrenched beliefs into more positive ones

Sources Of Negative Beliefs

Understanding where negative core beliefs originate is essential for challenging and re-framing them. These beliefs are often deeply embedded in us from early family dynamics.

Families play a significant role in shaping how we see ourselves. Parental expectations, whether spoken or unspoken, can have a lasting impact on our self-view. For example, if parents constantly demand perfection or show love conditionally based on achievements, children might internalize the belief that they are only worthy when excelling. Over time, this can lead to a pervasive sense of inadequacy or an endless pursuit of approval, leaving people feeling perpetually not good enough even in adulthood.

It can be easy to feel that core beliefs are impossible to change, but they aren't! With dedicated effort toward shifting them, incredible improvements can be made in how you think about yourself and what you believe. You can use this quick reflective quiz to help determine if childhood experiences led to negative internal beliefs:

1. When you were growing up, how did your caregivers express love and approval?
    a. Unconditionally, regardless of my achievements or behavior
    b. Mostly when I accomplished something or met expectations
    c. Rarely, or only in specific situations
    d. I'm not sure—it was unpredictable
2. If you made a mistake as a child, how did your family typically respond?
    a. They reassured me that mistakes were a natural part of learning
    b. They were disappointed, and I felt pressure to do better next time
    c. They were critical or made me feel ashamed
    d. Mistakes were not talked about, but I felt I had to be perfect
3. Which of these thoughts do you relate to most when reflecting on your childhood experiences?
    a. "I always felt accepted for who I was, no matter what."
    b. "I had to work hard to earn approval or love."
    c. "I often felt like I wasn't good enough, no matter how hard I tried."
    d. "I still don't know if I was ever truly accepted for just being me."
4. Did you ever feel that your worth was tied to your achievements, behavior, or how well you met expectations?
    a. No, I always felt valued regardless
    b. Sometimes—I noticed I got more attention when I did well

      c. Often—I felt that being perfect or successful was the only way to be loved

      d. Yes, I still feel this way even now

5. Looking at your current self-talk, do you ever catch yourself thinking things like…

      a. "I am enough as I am, no matter what I do."

      b. "If I don't succeed, people will think less of me."

      c. "I have to be perfect to be worthy of love."

      d. "I'm constantly seeking approval, but it never feels like enough."

If you answered mostly b, c, or d, it may indicate that early experiences shaped negative core beliefs related to self-worth, perfectionism, or approval-seeking. These beliefs, while deeply ingrained, can be challenged and reframed through self-compassion and intentional healing work.

Furthermore, societal influences have a big impact when it comes to forming core beliefs. Society bombards us with standards around success, beauty, and behavior, often portrayed through media, culture, and community norms. These external pressures can conflict with personal identities and values, which in turn can lead to a distorted self-perception. Take beauty standards, for example; when society glorifies a narrow definition of beauty, those who don't fit that mold may develop negative beliefs about their appearance.

Constant comparison to unrealistic ideals enables a sense of failure to develop, as people feel they must conform to be accepted and appreciated. This exercise will help you reflect on the societal messages you've absorbed and challenge any negative core beliefs they may have created:

1. **Step 1: Recognize Societal Messages.** Take a few moments to think about the messages you've received from media, culture, and society about success, beauty, and behavior. Then, answer the following:

    a. Success: What did society teach you about what it means to be "successful"?

    ----

    b. Beauty: What beauty standards were you exposed to?

_____
_____
_____

c. Behavior: What messages did you receive about how you "should" act?

_____
_____
_____

2. **Step 2: Identify the Impact on Your Beliefs.** Now, consider how these societal messages may have shaped your self-perception. Ask yourself:

   a. Which of these messages have I internalized?

   _____
   _____
   _____

   b. Do these beliefs align with my personal values?

   _____
   _____
   _____

   c. How has this belief affected my self-worth?

   _____
   _____
   _____

3. **Step 3: Challenge and Reframe the Beliefs.** For each negative belief you've identified, write a new, self-compassionate belief that aligns with your true values.

   _____
   _____
   _____
   _____
   _____

4. **Step 4: Take Action to Reinforce New Beliefs.** Think of one small action you can take to affirm your new belief. This might be:

   a. Unfollowing social media accounts that promote unrealistic standards

   b. Practicing self-affirmations

   c. Surrounding yourself with people who value you beyond societal expectations

5. **Step 5: Reflect.** Journal about how this exercise made you feel. Were there any beliefs that surprised you? How can you continue challenging societal influences in your daily life?

_____
_____
_____
_____
_____

Traumatic experiences also shape our beliefs about self-worth and capability. Trauma, whether from abuse, neglect, or extreme stress, often instills harmful notions about oneself. People who endure trauma might come to see themselves as damaged or undeserving of positive experiences, a symptom frequently linked with long-term mental health challenges like anxiety or depression. The cognitive-emotional processing of trauma impacts how these beliefs form and persist. According to cognitive theories, negative post-traumatic cognitions depict perceptions of helplessness and worthlessness (Punamäki et al., 2018). Such ingrained beliefs create barriers to recognizing your potential and celebrating personal strengths.

Impact On Daily Life

Negative core beliefs are deeply entrenched perceptions that can create significant barriers across multiple aspects of life. While these beliefs might go unnoticed, their impact is pervasive, subtly influencing how we view ourselves and interact with the world around us.

Beginning with self-esteem, the internalization of negative core beliefs can diminish your sense of self worth and lead to feelings of inadequacy. For example, if you repeatedly hear or believe you are not good enough, this belief can become deeply ingrained and affect your confidence and how you perceive your abilities in various situations. You can use this activity to help you question negative core beliefs:

1. **Step 1: Identify a Negative Core Belief:** Write down a belief that diminishes your self-esteem (e.g., "I'm not good enough.").

_____

_____

_____

2. **Step 2: Question Its Origins:** Ask yourself: Where did this belief come from? Who or what reinforced it?

   _____

   _____

   _____

3. **Step 3: Challenge the Belief:** What evidence supports this belief? What evidence contradicts it? What would I tell a friend who felt this way?

   _____

   _____

   _____

4. **Step 4: Reframe It:** Rewrite the belief in a self-compassionate way (e.g., "I am worthy as I am, and I am always growing.").

   _____

   _____

   _____

5. **Step 5: Take Action:** Do one small thing today that reinforces your new belief (e.g., say an affirmation, set a boundary, or engage in a confidence-building activity).

Furthermore, decision-making processes are shaped by these beliefs. Negative core beliefs function as invisible filters through which people interpret their choices and experiences. When someone holds a belief that they will inevitably fail, it can prevent them from taking risks or exploring new ventures. This often leads to stagnation, as people become trapped in cycles of self-doubt and indecision. If you want to begin working toward eliminating self-doubt in decision-making, give this activity a try:

1. **Recall a Recent Hesitation:** Think of a decision you avoided or struggled with. What fear or doubt held you back?
2. **Identify the Underlying Belief:** What thought influenced your hesitation? (e.g., "I always make the wrong choice.")
3. **Shift Perspective:** Imagine advising a friend in your situation. What would you tell them?
4. **Reframe the Belief:** Replace the negative thought with a more empowering one (e.g., "Every choice is a learning experience.").

5. **Take a Small Step:** Do one thing today that moves you forward, even if it is just exploring an option.

In addition, negative core beliefs can pose significant impediments to romantic relationships. The belief of being unworthy of love or affection can lead to unhealthy relational patterns, where you either overly accommodate others to gain approval or withdraw to protect yourself from anticipated rejection. This impedes authentic connections, as relationships become built on a faulty foundation of perceived inadequacy rather than mutual respect and understanding.

The inability to trust or open up fully puts strain on partnerships and friendships, often leading to misunderstandings or prolonged conflicts. With this activity, you can start to unravel how these beliefs impact trust in your relationships:

1. **Reflect on Past Patterns:** Think about your relationships. Do you tend to over-accommodate, withdraw, or struggle with trust? Write down a specific example.
2. **Identify the Root Belief:** What underlying thought drives this pattern? (e.g., "If I open up, I will be rejected." or "I have to earn love by meeting others' needs.")
3. **Assess the Impact on Trust:** Ask yourself:
    a. How does this belief affect my ability to trust others?
    b. Have I misinterpreted support as rejection or distance as disinterest?
    c. How have these assumptions shaped my connections?
4. **Consider an Alternative View:** What if the belief isn't entirely true? How might your relationships look if trust was based on reality rather than fear?
5. **Take a Small Step Toward Trust:** Choose one action to test a new approach—share a small vulnerability, set a boundary, or communicate a need.

Strategies For Change

Identifying and shifting negative core beliefs is a necessary step toward healing and personal growth. An effective approach to achieving this is through cognitive restructuring, a technique rooted in cognitive behavioral therapy (CBT). This involves critically assessing and challenging irrational thoughts that contribute to harmful beliefs.

Questioning the validity of these thoughts means that you can begin to reshape your perceptions, leading to healthier mental patterns (Stanborough, 2023).

Self-monitoring is a simple, practical way that you can begin this process, which works like so:

1. **Step 1: Start a Thought Journal:** Carry a small notebook or use a digital app to jot down negative thoughts as they occur throughout your day. Try to capture the exact thought, not just the feeling. For example: "I will never be good enough."
2. **Step 2: Identify Recurring Patterns:** After a few days, review your notes and look for patterns or triggers. Are there specific situations or people that bring up certain negative beliefs?
3. **Step 3: Challenge the Thoughts:** When you notice a recurring thought, pause and ask yourself:
    a. "Is this thought based on facts or assumptions?"
    b. "What evidence do I have to support or refute this belief?"
    c. "If I'm wrong, what is a more balanced perspective?"
4. **Step 4: Reframe the Thought:** Create a new, more realistic (or compassionate) thought to replace the negative one. For example, replace "I will never be good enough" with "I have strengths and I'm always growing."
5. **Step 5: Practice Consistently:** Each time you catch a negative thought, repeat the process of questioning and reframing. Over time, this will become a habit, helping you gradually shift away from negative thinking patterns.

Another tool is the use of affirmations. These are positive statements aimed at counteracting negative self-talk, thereby reinforcing a stronger self-image. The repetition of affirmations can gradually shift your focus from self-doubt to self-empowerment. For example, if your negative belief is "I'm not good enough," an affirmation could be, "I am capable and worthy of success."

Mindfulness practices are another valuable strategy for addressing negative core beliefs. Mindfulness enhances awareness of unhelpful thought patterns, which allows you to observe your thoughts without immediate reaction. This practice encourages emotional regulation and fosters a sense of peace and acceptance.

To incorporate mindfulness into your daily routine, set aside time each day to practice mindful breathing or meditation. Start with just five minutes of focusing on your breath, noticing how it feels as it flows in and out of your body. Should any negative thoughts or emotions arise, acknowledge them without judgment, and gently redirect your focus back to your breath. Over time, mindfulness can help reduce the impact of negative beliefs on your mood and behavior, promoting greater emotional balance.

Also, integrating mindfulness into everyday activities can be helpful. Try paying full attention to mundane tasks like washing dishes or walking, fully engaging your senses and mind in the present moment. As you become more attuned to your internal experiences, you gain insight into how thoughts influence emotions, as well as opportunities to challenge and alter these patterns.

Moving Forward

In this chapter, we've discussed the many roots of negative core beliefs and how they affect our daily lives. Recognizing how these beliefs stem from early family influences, societal pressures, and even personal relationships helps us understand why they feel so ingrained.

Now, it's time to focus on change. We've shared strategies like cognitive restructuring, affirmations, and mindfulness, which can all play a significant role in reshaping negative beliefs. These tools help you question and reshape harmful thoughts, which in turn encourages healthier perspectives. Remember, every small step toward change matters.

Chapter Three

REFRAMING EXERCISES—HEALING CHILDHOOD WOUNDS

Reframing exercises are a helpful method to address the lingering impact of childhood wounds. They help us understand how to reshape how we view and process painful memories, offering a fresh perspective that can lead to healing. These exercises do not seek to erase the past; rather, they help us reinterpret our experiences in a way that empowers us.

In this chapter, we'll explore various exercises designed to change your relationship with traumatic experiences. You'll learn practical techniques for shifting negative perceptions, which include identifying and altering destructive thought patterns. We will discuss how changing your narrative can reduce feelings of shame and increase your ability to cope with future challenges.

This chapter will also address common misconceptions about reframing, ensuring you understand its purpose and potential benefits.

Understanding Reframing

We've talked about reframing before, but now it's time to dive deeper. Reframing is a powerful therapeutic tool that can change how we view our past experiences, particularly those involving trauma. To be clear, it's not just a matter of changing the way we think; it centers around changing the narrative of our own stories to help heal old wounds and improve resilience. To understand the significance of reframing, let's break it down into its essential components.

First, what exactly is reframing in a therapeutic context? Reframing is a technique used to shift the perspective through which we view certain events or experiences. It involves taking a negative event or thought and transforming it into a more positive or neutral interpretation. This doesn't mean denying the reality of what happened; instead, it means altering our understanding and emotional response to that reality. For example, if someone felt inadequate due to a challenging childhood experience, reframing would involve exploring how those feelings could act as a driving force for personal growth and self-discovery.

In order to work with reframing your experiences through multiple different interpretations, work through this activity to reframe an experience through the lens of a friend, a therapist or professional, and a neutral third party:

1. **Choose an Experience:** Reflect on a recent event or experience that triggered negative feelings or thoughts (e.g., a disagreement, a perceived failure, or a missed opportunity). Write it down briefly.

    ----

2. **Reframe Through the Lens of a Friend:** Imagine a close friend is telling you about the experience. What would they say to offer support or a different perspective?

    ----

3. **Reframe Through the Lens of a Therapist or Professional:** Consider how a therapist or professional might approach the situation. What insight or reframing might they offer to help you see things more objectively?

    ----

4. **Reframe Through the Lens of a Neutral Third-Party:** Imagine you are an outsider observing the situation with no emotional attachment. What might a neutral third party say to describe the event or offer a new perspective?

5. **Compare the Perspectives:** Look at how each perspective reframes the experience. How do these alternative views shift your understanding of the event? Write down any new insights or feelings you have after considering the different viewpoints.

Addressing common misconceptions about reframing is also important. Some people view reframing as a form of denial, thinking that by shifting focus away from painful aspects, they're ignoring the reality of their experiences. However, reframing is not about pretending something didn't happen or minimizing its impact. Rather, it is about acknowledging what occurred while choosing to interpret it in a way that serves your healing process positively. It is about empowerment and developing a new lens through which to view your past.

Implementing Positive Narratives

Focusing on creating and practicing positive self-narratives is important when it comes to reframing.

Affirmations

Crafting positive affirmations is one essential technique that can help transform your inner dialogue from critical to supportive. Developing affirmations that resonate personally can be a daily reminder of your worth and resilience. This involves simple but powerful statements like "I am capable" or "I am deserving of love," which counteract negative self-talk with acceptance and healing. These affirmations should be present-tense, personal, and positive to encourage a mindset shift over time.

Finding the right affirmations often requires experimentation. This activity can help you craft personalized affirmations to fit your needs when it comes to reframing traumatic experiences:

1. **Step 1: Identify the Core Issue.** Think about a traumatic experience or ongoing struggle that you want to reframe. Write down the core belief or feeling related to it (e.g., "I am not safe," "I will never heal," or "I am unworthy of love.").

    ----

2. **Step 2: Recognize Negative Patterns.** Reflect on the negative self-talk or recurring thoughts related to this experience. How does this belief affect your emotional well-being, behavior, or sense of self? Write these thoughts down (e.g., "I can't trust anyone" or "I always mess things up.").

    ----

3. **Step 3: Craft a Positive Affirmation.** Now, create an affirmation that directly challenges the negative belief. Focus on empowering, compassionate language that aligns with your healing goals. Make sure the affirmation feels achievable, even if it is not fully true yet.

    ----

4. **Step 4: Test the Affirmation.** Speak your affirmation out loud. How does it make you feel? Does it resonate, or does it feel too distant or unrealistic? If it feels hard to believe, modify the language to make it feel more attainable. For example, if "I am worthy of love" feels too difficult, try "I am learning to accept love in small ways."

   ----

5. **Step 5: Repeat and Adjust.** Practice your affirmation daily. If it doesn't feel powerful, adjust it. Try adding visualizations or writing the affirmation in a way that feels more aligned with your emotional state. As you continue, you may find that certain affirmations evolve and deepen as your healing progresses.

   ----

6. **Step 6: Reflect on Your Progress.** At the end of the week, reflect on any shifts in your mindset. Have you noticed any changes in how you perceive the traumatic experience or how you treat yourself? Write down any insights or improvements.

Storytelling

Storytelling as a healing tool invites us to use our personal narratives to harness connections and understanding, both internally and with others. Sharing your journey with someone safe allows vulnerability to emerge, which is necessary for empathy and healing.

1. **Step 1: Pick a Pivotal Moment.** Think of a defining event—big or small—that shaped you. Jot it down in a few sentences.

   ----

2. **Step 2: Tune Into the Emotions.** What emotions did this event stir? Fear, joy, sadness? Write them out as they come to you.

   _____

   _____

   _____

3. **Step 3: Share With Someone You Trust.** Find a safe listener—a friend, family member, or therapist—and share your story. Keep it raw and real by avoiding the urge to edit out uncomfortable details.

4. **Step 4: Invite Connection.** Ask your listener for empathy, not solutions. Just be present with your truth and let the vulnerability flow.

5. **Step 5: Reflect on the Shift.** How did telling your story feel? Lighter? Empowered? Write a quick note about the experience.

   _____

   _____

   _____

6. **Step 6: Make It a Ritual.** Consider sharing a part of your story regularly—through journaling or in conversation. Let storytelling become a tool for growth and connection.

Visualization

Visualizations for positive change are another effective technique in the healing toolkit. Guided visualizations help you envision yourself overcoming trauma by harboring positive desires and outcomes. This practice enhances belief in one's ability to heal and integrates positive experiences into the self-concept. For example, you can give this visualization exercise a try:

1. Sit or lie down in a comfortable place. Close your eyes and take a few deep breaths, releasing tension with each exhale.
2. Imagine yourself five years from now, fully healed and thriving. Visualize this version of you in vivid detail—how do you look, feel, and carry yourself? Where are you? What are you doing?

3. Your future self turns to you with a kind, knowing expression. What advice do they have for you? What words of reassurance or encouragement do they offer? Listen closely.
4. Picture yourself stepping into your future self's body. Feel their confidence, strength, and peace as if they are already yours. Let this feeling sink into your present moment.
5. Slowly return to the present while holding onto the emotions of empowerment and hope. Open your eyes and write down key takeaways—what stood out? What mindset shifts did you notice?

Repeat this visualization whenever you need motivation or reassurance. Over time, you will internalize this vision, making it easier to embody your healing journey.

Writing About Achievements

Writing about your achievements, no matter how small, consolidates progress and motivates further strides forward. Keep a success journal where you document instances of resilience, like standing up for yourself or making a positive decision. Revisiting these entries during challenging times reassures you of your capacity to overcome obstacles. Peer support groups, either in-person or virtual, also provide constructive feedback and allow members to celebrate milestones together, ensuring no victory goes unnoticed (Annie, 2021).

Integrating Past With Present

Reflective practices can bridge connecting past trauma with present healing, allowing you to turn deep-seated wounds into sources of strength and self-awareness.

Connecting The Dots

A practical approach to enhancing this self-awareness is through "Connecting the Dots" exercises. For example, this exercise can help you identify patterns between past experiences and current beliefs to increase self-awareness:

1. **Step 1: Identify a Core Belief.** Write down one negative core belief you hold about yourself (e.g., "I am not good enough" or "I can't trust others").

2. **Step 2: Trace It Back.** Ask yourself:

    a. Where did this belief originate?

    ----

    b. What early experiences reinforced it?

    ----

    c. Who or what influenced this belief (family, society, past relationships)?

    ----

3. **Step 3: Connect the Dots.** Draw a simple timeline or mind map linking past events that contributed to this belief. Note any recurring themes or patterns.

    ----

4. **Step 4: Challenge the Narrative.** Look at your timeline and ask:

    a. Are these past events definitive proof of my belief, or just isolated moments?

    ----

    b. How might someone else interpret these events differently?

    ----

5. **Step 5: Rewrite the Belief.** Craft a new, more balanced belief based on your reflections (e.g., "I am learning that my worth isn't based on perfection").

6. **Step 6: Apply It.** For the next week, when your old belief surfaces, replace it with your new, reframed perspective. Keep a log of how this shift impacts your thoughts and feelings.

Inner Child Dialogues

Engaging in healing dialogues with your inner child is another incredible option. This process involves writing letters to your younger self, acknowledging the pain, fears, and unmet needs experienced during those formative years. Through such letters, you offer compassion and understanding—elements perhaps absent during your real childhood. If you'd like to try this process now, you can use the space below to write:

Mindfulness Techniques

Mindfulness techniques can aid in integrating past traumas with present consciousness. These techniques can help you confront painful memories without being overwhelmed by them. Engaging in mindful breathing and body scans, for example, can help ground you in the present moment and allow you to observe your feelings or any sensations without attaching judgments or narratives to them. For example, try this mindful breathing exercise and then reflect on your experience in the space below:

1. Sit or lie down, close your eyes, and take a deep breath in through your nose.
2. Feel the air fill your lungs, then slowly exhale through your mouth.
3. Pay attention to the rise and fall of your chest. If thoughts come up, gently return to your breath.
4. Silently say: "Inhale, I am present. Exhale, I let go."
5. After a few minutes, open your eyes and note how you feel. More calm? Less tense?

Rituals for Healing

Creating rituals for healing further supports this integration process. Rituals need not be complex; they can be simple acts imbued with personal significance. For example, you can try lighting a candle each time you reflect on what you've learned or writing affirmations of strength and resilience in a journal dedicated to your healing journey. Such rituals honor the past while consciously rooting you in the present, providing a structured means of acknowledging trauma and celebrating progress.

The act of creating personal rituals imparts a sense of agency and control often lost in traumatic experiences. This worksheet is here to help you create personal rituals that are meaningful to you:

Date: _____

Step 1: Identify Your Intention

What do you want your ritual to focus on? (e.g., releasing pain, building self-compassion, celebrating progress)

_____
_____
_____
_____

Step 2: Choose a Simple Action

Select an act that feels meaningful to you:

- Lighting a candle
- Writing affirmations
- Placing a hand over your heart
- Drinking a cup of tea mindfully
- Other: _____

Step 3: Add Personal Meaning

How can you make this ritual feel special? (e.g., using a specific scent, a meaningful object, or a special time of day)

_____
_____
_____
_____

Step 4: Set a Time & Place

When and where will you practice this ritual? (e.g., every morning, before bed, during moments of stress)

_____
_____
_____
_____

Step 5: Reflect & Adjust

After practicing your ritual, write a few words about how it made you feel. Does it need any adjustments?

_____
_____
_____
_____

Moving Forward

As we wrap up this chapter, remember that reframing is not just a tool—it's a way of reshaping how you see your past and its impact on your life. Remember, by engaging in exercises that help you reframe traumatic experiences, you're taking steps toward healing and empowerment. This process encourages viewing past challenges as opportunities for growth rather than obstacles. Whether it's through changing your narrative or using affirmations to build a positive mindset, these techniques are about embracing your story in a healthier, more constructive way.

Chapter Four

INCORPORATING OTHER THERAPEUTIC APPROACHES—A HOLISTIC VIEW

Exploring complementary therapies can provide a more holistic view of treating emotional and psychological issues that you may have faced. More than just focusing on one method, combining different therapeutic approaches can enhance cognitive processing and offer broader support to those in need. With trauma often being complex and multifaceted, a singular approach might overlook crucial elements.

Integrating therapies not only addresses multiple dimensions of trauma but also opens up new avenues for recovery. It's like having a personalized toolkit where each tool serves a specific purpose, yet all work cohesively towards the same goal. This chapter delves into how these diverse therapies can act synergistically, enriching the healing process.

Benefits Of A Blended Approach

Incorporating personalized, blended therapeutic methods offers numerous advantages as you work toward recovery and healing from trauma. One of the most significant benefits is the customization of therapy according to individual needs, which can enhance both engagement and commitment, ultimately leading to better outcomes. A personalized approach means that the therapy is specifically tailored to address the unique challenges and strengths of each individual. This personalized attention helps create a more comfortable and relatable therapeutic environment where you feel understood and valued. As a result, you are more likely to actively participate and commit to your treatment plan, whether it was created by a professional or by yourself.

Which Therapy Is Right For You?

This chapter is here to help you see the benefits of two blended approaches: cognitive behavioral therapy (CBT) with eye movement desensitization and reprocessing (EMDR), and internal family systems (IFS) with dialectical behavioral therapy (DBT). While you can certainly use both of these blended approaches, it can be helpful to know where to start or which option to work with first. This simple guide can help you use easy criteria to determine which choice might be best for you:

- CBT + EMDR: Ideal if you struggle with intrusive thoughts, trauma triggers, or distressing memories.
    - Best for those who want a structured, goal-oriented approach.
    - Helps with reprocessing traumatic experiences to reduce emotional distress.
    - Useful if you often feel stuck in negative thought patterns or struggle with cognitive distortions.
    - Recommended if past trauma significantly impacts your daily life and functioning.
- IFS + DBT: Ideal if you experience intense emotions, internal conflicts, or difficulty with self-regulation.
    - Best for those who want to develop emotional resilience and self-compassion.
    - Helps you to understand and integrate different "parts" of yourself (e.g., inner critic, protector).
    - Useful if you struggle with overwhelming emotions, impulsivity, or difficulties in relationships.
    - Recommended if self-sabotaging behaviors or deep-seated emotional wounds interfere with healing.
- Combination Approach:
    - If both trauma processing and emotional regulation are priorities, integrating both methods may be beneficial.

- Starting with DBT skills can provide emotional stability before engaging in deeper trauma work with EMDR.
- IFS can help resolve internal conflicts that may arise when challenging negative thoughts in CBT.

Combining CBT And EMDR

The first combined approach I want to share with you is CBT alongside EMDR. Integrating CBT with EMDR is an incredible approach to addressing cognitive distortions and emotional trauma. Each therapy has its strengths, but when combined, they can address a wider range of issues simultaneously. CBT focuses on identifying and reshaping negative thought patterns.

On the other hand, EMDR uses bilateral stimulation techniques to aid in processing traumatic memories more effectively. This process reduces the emotional charge associated with painful memories, allowing clients to reprocess them without the intense emotional reactions previously experienced.

Combining CBT and EMDR not only facilitates faster symptom relief but also enhances long-term recovery success rates. The structured, goal-oriented nature of CBT provides a straightforward path for addressing immediate concerns by modifying dysfunctional thoughts and behaviors. When EMDR is integrated into this process, it offers an additional layer by targeting the deep-rooted emotional responses tied to traumatic memories. This dual approach helps in unblocking the psychological barriers that hinder healing.

Activities For Blending EMDR And CBT

While it can be helpful to engage in CBT or EMDR with a therapist, it's also understandable to not be ready for professional support, or to be unable to access it. Fortunately, both CBT and EMDR can be facilitated in a self-guided way, and these activities are here to help you blend the two.

ACTIVITY 1: THOUGHT REPROCESSING WITH BILATERAL STIMULATION

This activity is here to help you challenge negative thoughts while engaging in bilateral stimulation to reduce emotional distress.

1. **Identify a Distressing Thought:** Write down a negative thought related to a past trauma (e.g., "I am not safe" or "It was my fault").

   _____
   _____
   _____
   _____

2. **Challenge the Thought (CBT):** Ask yourself:

   a. What evidence supports this thought?

   _____
   _____
   _____

   b. What evidence contradicts it?

   _____
   _____
   _____

   c. What is a more balanced perspective?

   _____
   _____
   _____

3. **Engage in Bilateral Stimulation (EMDR-Inspired):** While focusing on your restructured thought, engage in one of the following:

   a. Tap your shoulders alternately left and right.

   b. Move your eyes from left to right for 30 seconds.

   c. Listen to alternating bilateral audio (use a free app or YouTube video).

4. **Reflect:** After completing the process, note any changes in how you feel about the thought. Repeat as needed.

   _____
   _____
   _____
   _____

ACTIVITY 2: SAFE PLACE VISUALIZATION WITH COGNITIVE RESTRUCTURING

With this activity, you can establish a mental "safe space" to counteract distressing thoughts and emotions.

1. **Create Your Safe Space:** Close your eyes and imagine a peaceful, secure place. It could be real or imaginary (such as a beach or a cozy cabin).
2. **Engage Your Senses:** What do you see, hear, smell, and feel in this place? Deepen the visualization by adding rich details.
3. **Introduce a Healing Thought (CBT):** Once grounded in this space, repeat a positive belief related to your healing (e.g., "I am safe now" or "I am strong").
4. **Add Bilateral Stimulation (EMDR-Inspired):** While visualizing and repeating your affirmation, tap gently on your knees or cross your arms and tap your shoulders alternately.
5. **Reflect:** After a few minutes, open your eyes and write about how you felt. Use this technique during moments of distress.

ACTIVITY 3: REWRITING THE NARRATIVE WITH EYE MOVEMENTS

With this activity, you can reprocess a difficult memory by rewriting the story while engaging in eye movements.

1. **Select a Memory:** Choose a past event that still carries emotional weight. Write a brief description.

    _____
    _____
    _____
    _____

2. **Identify the Negative Belief:** What belief formed from this memory? (e.g., "I am powerless" or "I don't deserve love").

    _____
    _____
    _____
    _____

3. **Rewrite the Narrative (CBT):** Imagine how a compassionate friend, mentor, or your future healed self would rewrite this story with a more empowering perspective.

    _____
    _____

----

4. **Engage in Eye Movements (EMDR-Inspired):** As you read the new version of your story, move your eyes left to right for 30 seconds or use gentle tapping.
5. **Reflect:** Write down any emotional shifts or new insights. Repeat as needed to reinforce the new perspective.

Exploring DBT And IFS For Trauma

If CBT and EMDR don't sound like a helpful combination, there's another approach that can focus on past traumas, coping tools, and similar exercises, rather than reprocessing and reframing.

DBT and IFS offer distinctive benefits when combined as well. This approach provides a comprehensive and supportive framework for individuals seeking to overcome past traumas and build healthier emotional lives.

DBT is renowned for its focus on teaching emotional regulation skills, which are essential for those of us who have experienced trauma. Often, trauma survivors struggle with intense emotions that might feel overwhelming or uncontrollable.

DBT introduces techniques that help recognize emotions without judgment, manage their intensity, and respond to them in healthier ways. For example, mindfulness practices, a core component of DBT, encourage us to stay present and aware of our emotions, reducing the tendency to act impulsively during distressing situations.

On the other hand, IFS offers a unique perspective by helping us explore our internal landscape, which consists of different "parts" that make up our personality. These parts are often created as protective mechanisms during traumatic experiences. Identifying these components can help you understand how they have functioned in their lives, often leading you to discover that what was once protective can now be limiting or harmful.

IFS encourages self-compassion and promotes understanding of personal experiences. For example, someone might recognize a part of themselves that becomes hyper-vigilant due to past trauma, and through IFS, they can learn to reassure this segment of themselves and integrate it healthily into their broader sense of self.

Activities For Blending DBT And IFS

Now, it's time for us to focus on activities that blend DBT and IFS for maximum benefits.

ACTIVITY 1: EMOTION MAPPING WITH YOUR INTERNAL PARTS

This activity helps you use DBT's emotional regulation techniques alongside IFS self-exploration to better understand and soothe your inner parts.

1. **Identify a Strong Emotion:** Think of a recent situation that triggered an intense emotion (e.g., anger, sadness, fear). Write it down.

   _____
   _____
   _____
   _____

2. **Locate the Emotion in Your Body:** Where do you feel it? (e.g., tight chest, clenched jaw, sinking stomach).

   _____
   _____
   _____
   _____
   _____

3. **Identify the Part (IFS-Inspired):** Ask yourself, "Which part of me is holding this emotion? What is its role?"

   _____
   _____
   _____
   _____

4. **Engage in a DBT Coping Skill:** Choose one:

a. Deep breathing (inhale 4 seconds, hold 4, exhale 6).

   b. Hold an ice cube or splash cold water on your face to ground yourself.

   c. Name 5 things you can see, hear, or feel to stay present.

5. **Confront the Part:** With a compassionate mindset, ask the part of yourself: "What do you need from me right now?"

   _____
   _____
   _____
   _____
   _____
   _____
   _____

6. **Reflect:** Write about any insights gained and how your emotional response shifted.

   _____
   _____
   _____
   _____
   _____
   _____

ACTIVITY 2: WISE SELF MEDITATION FOR BALANCING INNER PARTS

With this activity, you can strengthen your core "self" while fostering compassion for your inner parts.

1. **Find a Quiet Space:** Sit comfortably and close your eyes.
2. **Breathe and Center Yourself:** Take slow, deep breaths, allowing yourself to relax.
3. **Visualize Your Internal System:** Picture your different parts in a safe, open space (e.g., a circle, a cozy room).
4. **Call Forth Your Wise Self:** Imagine a calm, compassionate version of you stepping into the space.
5. **Greet Each Part:** One by one, acknowledge your parts (e.g., the Worrier, the Perfectionist, the Protector).
6. **Ask Each Part a Question:** "What are you trying to protect me from?" or "How can we work together?"

7. **End With Self-Compassion:** Thank each part for its role and reassure them that you are in control.

ACTIVITY 3: URGE SURFING WITH PARTS AWARENESS

With this activity, you can manage impulsive reactions (DBT) while recognizing the inner parts driving them (IFS).

1. **Identify a Current Urge:** This could be an urge to react impulsively, avoid something, or engage in self-sabotaging behavior.
2. **Pause & Name the Urge:** Say to yourself, "I feel an urge to [behavior], but I don't have to act on it."
3. **Notice the Part Behind It:** Ask, "Which part of me wants to do this? What is its goal?"
4. **Ride the Wave (DBT-Inspired):** Imagine the urge as a wave rising and falling. Instead of fighting it, watch it pass naturally.
5. **Soothe the Part:** Speak to it kindly, saying something like, "I see you. I understand you are trying to help me. Let's find another way."
6. **Choose a Healthy Alternative:** Engage in a self-soothing or grounding activity instead (e.g., journaling, walking, listening to music).

Moving Forward

In this chapter, we've dived into how combining different therapeutic models alongside one another can really power up the healing journey for those of us dealing with trauma. Each of the therapies that we discussed comes with its own unique strengths, but when blended, they tackle a broader spectrum of issues. Now, you know which combinations might be beneficial for you, as well as which activities you can work with to experience the benefits of a combined approach.

Chapter Five

ADDITIONAL EXERCISES—CBT, CPT, AND DBT

In the previous chapters, we explored how CBT, CPT, DBT, and EMDR can support healing from C-PTSD. In this chapter, we will build upon that foundation by introducing eight new activities from CBT, CPT, and DBT that can deepen your self-awareness, improve emotional regulation, and help shift negative core beliefs. These exercises are designed to be practical, accessible, and flexible enough to be integrated into your daily healing journey.

CBT Exercises

First, let's explore some additional CBT exercises that you can use to expand your awareness and efforts toward healing.

Activity 1: The "Thought Ladder"

This activity is here to help you transform extreme negative thoughts into more balanced, constructive ones.

1. Write down a distressing thought (e.g., "I am completely unlovable").

_____
_____
_____
_____

2. Identify and write down a neutral, more balanced thought that is slightly closer to reality (e.g., "Some people have cared about me in the past").

    _____
    _____
    _____
    _____

3. Continue writing small, incremental steps toward a fully positive and realistic thought (e.g., "I have qualities that make me lovable" becomes "I am worthy of love and connection").

    _____
    _____
    _____
    _____

Repeat this practice when you notice self-defeating thoughts, gradually replacing them with more empowering beliefs.

ACTIVITY 2: "WHAT'S THE WORST THAT COULD HAPPEN?"

In recovery, it's often easy to worry about worst-case outcomes. However, this can hold us back because when we spend too much time worrying about impossible or odd outcomes, we don't devote time to taking healthy risks that lead to growth. With this exercise, you can reduce anxiety by exploring exaggerated fears logically.

1. Identify a situation that triggers fear or anxiety (e.g., "If I set a boundary, my friend will abandon me").

    _____
    _____
    _____
    _____

2. Ask yourself, "What's the absolute worst thing that could happen?" Write it down.

    _____
    _____

3. Next, ask, "What's the best possible outcome?" Write this down as well.

   _____
   _____
   _____
   _____

4. Finally, determine the most likely outcome, balancing both perspectives.

   _____
   _____
   _____
   _____

5. Reflect on how catastrophizing contributes to stress and how reality often lands somewhere in between extremes.

   _____
   _____
   _____
   _____
   _____

CPT Exercises

Next, we have some exercises that can help you put CPT techniques to good use, as we discussed previously.

Activity 1: The "Compassion Letter"

Reframing self-blame is an important part of healing from trauma, as many of us can wrongfully assume that certain events are our own fault. With this activity, you can reframe self-blame by writing to yourself with compassion.

1. Think about an event where you felt guilt, shame, or self-blame.
2. Imagine you are writing a letter to a close friend who went through the same experience.

3. Express understanding, kindness, and support in the letter. Reframe self-blame with empathy (e.g., "You did your best in that moment with what you knew"). Write your letter below.

_____
_____
_____
_____
_____
_____
_____
_____
_____
_____
_____
_____

Read the letter aloud or return to it when you need a reminder of your own strength and worth.

Activity 2: "Rewriting The Ending"

Restructuring a painful memory by giving it a new, healing resolution is an incredible way to strengthen your healing process. With this activity, you can accomplish this restructuring.

1. Choose a traumatic or distressing memory.
2. Write a detailed account of the memory as you recall it.

_____
_____
_____
_____
_____
_____

3. Now, rewrite the memory, imagining an alternative version where you receive support, protection, or agency over the situation.

4. Reflect on how this new narrative helps lessen the emotional charge of the original event.

DBT Exercises

DBT exercises are great for emotional regulation when it comes to C-PTSD healing. These DBT exercises can help you achieve better regulation and a sense of peace as you navigate the healing process.

Activity 1: "Turning Emotional Waves Into Messages"

This activity can help you develop emotional intelligence by interpreting emotions as information rather than threats.

1. Identify an intense emotion you've recently felt (e.g., anger, sadness, fear).

2. Ask yourself, "What is this emotion trying to tell me?" (e.g., "My anger is signaling that I feel disrespected").

_____
_____
_____
_____

3. List potential healthy responses to the emotion rather than reacting impulsively.

_____
_____
_____
_____

4. Over time, observe patterns in how emotions guide your needs and boundaries.

_____
_____
_____
_____

Activity 2: "Radical Acceptance Mind Map"

Radical acceptance is a method in DBT that aims to reduce anxiety and stress by allowing you to accept that some things are out of your control. To work with radical acceptance, you can use this activity—all you need is a blank piece of paper and a willingness to heal.

1. Draw a large circle in the center of a page and write "What I Can Control."
2. Around it, write specific actions you can take to improve your situation.
3. Outside the circle, write "What I Cannot Control" and list external factors beyond your influence.

Whenever you feel overwhelmed, revisit this map to focus on what is within your power.

Activity 3: "Opposite Action Practice"

This activity can help reduce emotional intensity by encouraging you to act opposite to unhelpful impulses.

1. Identify an emotion-driven impulse that does not serve you (e.g., withdrawing when feeling anxious).
2. Choose the opposite action that aligns with long-term well-being (e.g., reaching out to a trusted friend instead).
3. Practice consciously choosing opposite actions when emotional distress arises.
4. Track how this shift in behavior impacts your emotional state over time. You can use the space below for this.

Over time, use this framework to make intentional decisions that reinforce self-worth and empowerment.

Moving Forward

These activities provide new ways to engage with CBT, CPT, and DBT for deeper healing and self-awareness. Recovery is not a linear journey, and setbacks do not erase progress. The goal of these exercises is to offer a variety of tools you can lean on, depending on your needs at any given moment. Healing from C-PTSD is a process of self-discovery, growth, and reclaiming agency over your life. Keep moving forward, one step at a time.

Conclusion

Healing from complex PTSD is not a linear process, nor is it a one-size-fits-all experience. Throughout this book, you have explored a variety of therapeutic approaches and practical exercises designed to support your healing journey. Engaging in these activities shows that you have taken meaningful steps toward understanding yourself, reshaping negative thought patterns, and developing emotional resilience.

Remember, healing is a continuous process that requires patience and self-compassion. The tools you have practiced here can provide guidance and help you navigate challenges with greater confidence and clarity. As you move forward, continue to honor your progress, seek support when needed, and trust in your ability to reclaim your sense of self and well-being. You are not alone, and your journey toward healing is evidence of your strength and courage.

Book Four

THE POWER OF EMDR FOR C-PTSD RECOVERY

Introduction

Healing from C-PTSD is a deeply personal journey—one that requires a toolkit of therapies and techniques tailored to your unique needs. EMDR adds another layer of healing to your journey by targeting the emotional and physiological responses tied to traumatic memories.

At first, EMDR can feel intimidating. It's a complex process at a glance, which can make it feel inaccessible. However, this isn't the case at all; EMDR can be self-guided and maintain effectiveness, bringing you real and clear benefits as you work toward healing and living the life you deserve.

For women like you and I, EMDR can be incredible. But don't just take it from me; there are many women who can attest to the power of EMDR, such as my friend Natalia. When I asked her to talk about her experience with EMDR, she told me this:

> *EMDR was described to me as a way to dislodge trauma that got almost stuck in the brain, so it didn't process "correctly." This made it harder for me to cope because symptoms of trauma were making a big impact on my life. After working with self-guided EMDR consistently, though, that changed. I committed to the exercises and made a true effort, using visualization and bilateral stimulation, and I'm so glad I dedicated time to it! Now, situations that used to make me so anxious don't seem as bad anymore, and I feel more confident with addressing bigger experiences now too.*

Whether you're just beginning your EMDR journey or looking to deepen its impact, this book will provide you with a strong foundation in the principles of EMDR, along with step-by-step exercises to practice on your own or with a therapist. You'll also learn how to combine EMDR with other techniques to help you develop a comprehensive and effective healing routine. Through this exploration, we will uncover how EMDR can facilitate emotional release, unlock the body's innate healing potential, and empower you to reclaim a sense of safety, stability, and inner peace.

Let's take this next step toward integration, understanding, and healing together.

Chapter One

INTRODUCTION TO EMDR: THE BASICS

EMDR shows promise in the world of trauma recovery. It engages the mind differently than traditional talk therapy, offering hope and potential relief for those of us carrying the weight of uncomfortable memories due to C-PTSD. As we dig into this chapter, we'll talk about the fundamental concepts behind EMDR therapy and the different techniques involved. Understanding these basics grants you insight into how EMDR can be tailored to your needs, improving its effectiveness and comfort during sessions.

Understanding The Basics Of Eye Movement Techniques

At its core, EMDR uses specific eye movements to help you access and reprocess painful memories safely. When you experience trauma, these memories can become "stuck," which can overwhelm you with distressing emotions and physiological responses. Eye movement techniques come into play by facilitating access to these traumatic memories.

How EMDR Aids Trauma Recovery

The benefits of EMDR extend beyond memory reprocessing, offering substantial relief from psychological distress. It promotes emotional stability by helping people regain control over feelings linked to their traumatic pasts. When someone experiences trauma, their emotional responses can often be overwhelming and difficult to manage. EMDR introduces techniques that help stabilize these emotions (Moonraker Support, 2024). For example, if a person frequently experiences anxiety or panic attacks due to past trauma, EMDR can aid in diminishing these reactions by gradually desensitizing the emotional charge associated with certain memories.

Another function of EMDR lies in encouraging the integration of positive beliefs. Trauma often leaves us stranded in a web of negative self-perceptions, undermining our confidence and overall mental health as a result. EMDR helps replace these negative narratives with healthier, more adaptive thinking patterns, similar to cognitive reframing in CBT practices. To get yourself in the right mindset, use the space below. Jot down one negative thought you hold due to a past experience, and the healthier thought you'd like to eventually replace it. Keep this in mind as you explore EMDR; you'll find techniques that can help you integrate this more positive mindset.

_____
_____
_____
_____
_____
_____

EMDR Fit Assessment

While EMDR can be used by anyone, it's better suited to people who have specific circumstances surrounding their trauma, or who are more naturally inclined toward EMDR techniques in some way. This assessment is here to offer you some insight regarding whether EMDR is a right fit for you:

- Have you experienced trauma that feels "stuck" or difficult to process?
- Are you open to integrating physical and emotional experiences in therapy?
- Do you find it challenging to verbalize or fully access certain traumatic memories?
- Are you looking for a structured, goal-oriented therapy?

- Do you have a history of dissociation or emotional numbing?
- Are you currently working with a therapist, or are you comfortable with therapy that requires a collaborative approach?
- Do you experience frequent flashbacks, nightmares, or intrusive thoughts related to trauma?
- Are you open to exploring other therapeutic modalities alongside EMDR?

If you answered "yes" to even half of those questions, EMDR likely has something to offer you. As we continue on, you'll discover exactly how you can put EMDR to work.

Moving Forward

This chapter has unpacked the fundamental aspects of EMDR therapy, including the ways eye movement techniques work to unlock and reprocess those tough memories that can weigh heavily on our hearts. By using bilateral stimulation, you can navigate through traumatic experiences without being overwhelmed by the emotional waves they once triggered.

Chapter Two

PREPARING FOR EMDR—WHAT WOMEN NEED TO KNOW

Preparing for EMDR involves more than just deciding to tackle trauma; it also involves understanding what lies ahead in the therapy process. For many women seeking healing from past experiences, beginning EMDR is a deliberate step toward growth and recovery. It's normal to feel a mix of eagerness and apprehension when contemplating this therapeutic journey. After all, EMDR's approach is unique. This chapter invites you to explore these preparatory steps, ensuring that your introduction to EMDR feels less daunting and more like an empowering opportunity to regain control over your narrative.

Setting Realistic Expectations

When considering EMDR therapy, it's important to approach the process with a clear mindset by setting realistic expectations. Many people begin EMDR with hopes of quick results, but understanding the nature of EMDR can set the stage for a more fruitful experience.

Understanding How EMDR Works

First, it's important to recognize that EMDR is not a magic cure; it's a structured process requiring multiple sessions. Unlike treatments that may offer immediate relief but not lasting change, EMDR aims to address deeply ingrained trauma, which inherently takes time (Kaufman, 2024). Each session peels back layers of experiences, allowing for gradual healing. The eight phases of EMDR are systematically designed to facilitate this healing, with each phase playing a vital role in preparation and processing. Acknowledging that healing requires effort over an extended period ensures that women are better prepared for the commitment involved. This understanding helps to prevent discouragement if progress feels slow at times, reinforcing the idea that true healing is a journey rather than a destination.

ACTIVITY: SETTING REALISTIC EXPECTATIONS FOR YOUR EMDR JOURNEY

This activity will help you develop a clear and grounded understanding of the EMDR process and set realistic expectations to prevent discouragement throughout the EMDR experience.

1. **Understanding the Process:** Write down what you currently believe about trauma healing and EMDR. Reflect on any expectations you have about how quickly or easily you will heal. Are there any assumptions that healing should be immediate?

    _____
    _____
    _____

2. **The Layered Healing Approach:** On a blank page, draw an onion, rose, or spiral, to symbolize the layers of trauma processing. Label each layer with different aspects of healing (e.g., "Building Safety," "Processing Memories," "Strengthening Coping Skills," "Reframing Negative Beliefs," etc.). Acknowledge that healing happens in layers—some sessions may feel more productive than others, but each step is important.

3. **The EMDR Timeline:** On another page, create a flexible timeline for your healing journey. Instead of setting rigid deadlines, write down general milestones you'd like to reach (e.g., "Feel more comfortable discussing my trauma," "Experience fewer intrusive thoughts," "Feel more connected to my body"). Next to each milestone, note that healing progress is nonlinear, and setbacks are a normal part of growth.

4. **Commitment to the Journey:** Write a short personal affirmation, such as, "I acknowledge that healing takes time. I will be patient and compassionate with myself. Every step forward, no matter how small, is part of my transformation." Keep this affirmation somewhere visible to remind yourself of your commitment to steady, long-term healing.

   _____
   _____
   _____

Preparing For Emotional Responses

Emotional responses during EMDR therapy can be varied and sometimes unexpected. As EMDR works on reprocessing traumatic memories, emotions that have been suppressed or forgotten might resurface. Anticipating this range of responses is important, as it prepares you for the inevitable ups and downs of this therapy. To help you better anticipate and prepare for potential emotional responses that can arise during EMDR therapy, work through this activity:

1. **List Possible Emotional Responses:** Write down emotions you might experience during EMDR (e.g., sadness, fear, anger, relief).

   _____
   _____
   _____
   _____

2. **Identify Personal Triggers:** Next to each emotion, jot down potential triggers (e.g., "Fear = revisiting past abandonment").

   _____
   _____
   _____
   _____

3. **Plan Coping Strategies:** Beside each trigger, list a coping technique (e.g., deep breathing, grounding, journaling).

   _____
   _____
   _____
   _____

4. **Create a Safety Statement:** Write an affirmation to remind yourself of your strength, such as: "I trust this process. My emotions are valid and temporary. I am safe."

   _____
   _____
   _____
   _____

5. **Post-Session Reflection Prompt:** After a session, quickly note:

   a. What emotions surfaced?

   _____
   _____
   _____

   b. What helped me stay grounded?

   _____
   _____
   _____

   c. What will I do for self-care today?

   _____
   _____
   _____

Avoiding Comparison

Each woman's journey through EMDR is uniquely personal. It's easy to compare yourself to others, especially in group therapy settings or online forums where success stories are shared. However, it's important to remember that everyone's path through EMDR is different and influenced by their distinct experiences and emotional makeup. There's no one-size-fits-all timeline for healing. Instead of comparing your progress to others', focus on how far you've come since starting therapy. Success should be measured in personal milestones, no matter how small they may seem (Ascension Counseling, Ltd., 2024).

To recognize and appreciate personal successes in EMDR therapy without comparison to others, different activities can be helpful. This is one of my favorite activities to work through to achieve this:

1. **Define Success for Yourself:** Write down what healing success means to you—not based on others' experiences, but on your own growth.

   _____
   _____
   _____
   _____

2. **Create a "Wins" Jar or List:** Each week, write down one small achievement in your healing journey. If using a jar, fold each note and add it inside; if using a list, review it weekly.

   _____
   _____
   _____
   _____

3. **Gratitude for Growth:** Write a short reflection: "I am proud of myself for…"

   _____
   _____
   _____
   _____

4. **Affirmation Against Comparison:** Choose or create a personal affirmation, such as: "My healing is my own, and every step forward is a victory." Repeat it whenever the urge to compare yourself to others arises.

   _____
   _____
   _____
   _____
   _____
   _____
   _____

Having A Safety Net

Furthermore, before beginning EMDR, establishing a robust support network can significantly improve your emotional stability and therapeutic outcomes. Going into therapy with a safety net already in place provides an additional layer of security. This can include organizing regular check-ins with loved ones, participating in peer support groups, or engaging in activities that promote well-being.

Selecting A Qualified Therapist

Preparing yourself for EMDR also includes finding the right EMDR therapist, as finding the right therapist is a significant step for anyone considering this form of therapy. Working to prepare yourself is good, but finding a qualified therapist takes those efforts to the next level. While you can work with EMDR in a self-guided way, if you're looking to work with a professional, it's necessary to ensure that your therapist is adequately equipped to guide you through this healing journey. Begin by verifying their credentials. Check if they are licensed and have completed specialized training in EMDR, as these qualifications are fundamental for effective treatment. You can typically find this information on professional websites or by directly asking potential therapists.

When you are deciding on a therapist, prioritize those with trauma-specific experience. Therapists who regularly work with trauma-related issues will likely understand your unique situation better. Experience matters significantly, as it can considerably impact the effectiveness of your treatment.

Once you've shortlisted a few therapists, arrange for an initial consultation. This is your opportunity to gauge compatibility with your therapist. The importance of feeling comfortable and establishing trust is truly significant. A good therapeutic relationship is the foundation of successful therapy. During this meeting, ask about the therapist's approach to EMDR and how it might fit into a broader treatment plan. Discussing these specifics early on helps set realistic expectations and aligns both parties on the therapeutic goals. Inquire about how they plan to tackle your particular issues, whether it's PTSD, anxiety, or other conditions (jewaldrop925, 2023). During your initial consultation, ask the therapist the following questions and note their responses to help you gauge if they're a good fit:

- Are you certified or trained in EMDR?
- How many clients have you treated with EMDR?
- How do you integrate EMDR with other therapies?
- What is your approach to handling strong emotional responses during sessions?
- What is your communication style?

- How do you support clients between sessions if they struggle with processing?
- How long does a typical EMDR treatment plan last?
- How do you track progress in therapy?

Then, after a session, ask yourself the following:

- Did I feel heard and understood during our conversation?
- Do I feel safe and comfortable discussing my trauma with this therapist?

_____
_____
_____
_____

Additional Activities For Preparation

Because EMDR can bring up a lot of serious emotions, it's helpful to be prepared to manage emotions and support yourself through the process. Difficult emotions shouldn't discourage you from trying EMDR if you think it might be helpful; these emotions can be managed with preparation. Specifically, preparing helps you know what to expect and deal with anything that arises during an EMDR session. The following activities are here to guide you.

Identifying Your Trauma Narratives

Understanding the specific narratives tied to your trauma can be a great step in preparing for EMDR. This activity helps you pinpoint the stories you hold about yourself in relation to your traumatic experiences.

1. Reflect on key memories from your past that continue to evoke distress.
2. For each memory, note the story you tell yourself about it. Examples might include, "*I was abandoned,*" "*I am not good enough,*" or "*I am unworthy of love.*"
3. Write these down and think about how they have shaped your sense of self and your interactions with others.

_____
_____
_____

_____
_____
_____

This exercise helps you create a clearer picture of the negative beliefs you might wish to address in future EMDR sessions.

Visualizing Emotional Relief

One of the core benefits of EMDR is emotional desensitization and relief from distressing memories. This visualization exercise can help you build a sense of emotional safety and readiness for reprocessing.

1. Close your eyes and take a few deep, calming breaths.
2. Visualize a safe place where you feel at peace. This could be a location from your past or an imagined space that feels secure and comforting.
3. Focus on the physical sensations of being in this safe place (the sounds, smells, textures). Allow these sensations to ground you and create a feeling of calm.
4. Imagine the distressing memories you carry being gently lifted from your mind like leaves floating on a river, carried away by the current.
5. Sit in this peaceful state for several minutes, allowing your body and mind to relax.

This exercise helps you develop a positive emotional anchor to return to when you experience discomfort during or after EMDR processing.

Building Self-Compassion Through Affirmations

Replacing negative self-beliefs with positive ones is a key part of EMDR. You can work with this activity to begin the process of integrating healthier, compassionate thoughts into your everyday mindset.

1. Write down a list of negative beliefs or self-judgments you hold (e.g., "*I am not enough,*" "*I am broken*").

_____
_____

2. For each belief, create a compassionate, affirmative statement to replace it.

   _____
   _____
   _____
   _____

3. Say each affirmation out loud or write it down daily, focusing on how it makes you feel. You can even place these affirmations where you can see them every day (e.g., on your mirror, in your planner, etc.).

Using affirmations consistently can help gradually reshape the negative narratives tied to your trauma while preparing you for the cognitive shifts that will occur during EMDR.

Exploring Your Emotional Landscape

Sometimes, trauma manifests not just in memories but in ongoing emotional states. This activity helps you identify and understand the emotions that arise from your trauma, which makes space for greater self-awareness and emotional processing.

1. Set aside some quiet time each day for a few days to check in with your emotions.
2. Rate the intensity of each emotion you experience on a scale from 1 to 10 (1 being minimal, 10 being overwhelming).

   _____
   _____
   _____
   _____

3. Note when specific emotions arise. Are they connected to certain situations, memories, or triggers?

   _____
   _____
   _____
   _____

4. Write down any patterns you notice and explore how your emotions relate to your trauma history.

This activity supports ongoing emotional regulation by helping you recognize and acknowledge how past trauma continues to affect your emotional responses.

Creating A "Healing Resources" List

As you engage in EMDR, it's helpful to have a list of tools and resources to support your emotional and mental well-being between sessions. This activity encourages you to build your personal toolkit for healing.

1. In the space below, make a list of healing resources that work for you. These might include:
    a. Self-soothing techniques (deep breathing, holding a comforting object)
    b. Grounding practices (walking barefoot outside, mindfulness exercises)
    c. Supportive people or communities (friends, support groups, online forums)
    d. Creative outlets (journaling, drawing, music)
2. Keep your list handy for moments when you need support or relief between EMDR sessions.

Moving Forward

As you explore the process of preparing for EMDR, it's important to keep in mind that everyone's journey is unique. This chapter has emphasized setting realistic expectations and understanding the complexities involved. Grasping the nature of EMDR and recognizing that healing takes time means you are better equipped to dive into therapy with patience and resilience. It's not about comparing your progress to others but celebrating personal milestones along the way.

Chapter Three

REFRAMING AND CONNECTION— INTEGRATING EMDR WITH OTHER TECHNIQUES

Combining EMDR with other therapeutic techniques opens a world of possibilities for enhancing trauma recovery. This chapter dives into how reframing and connection are used to integrate these approaches. Inside, you'll learn about combining mindfulness with EMDR therapy, exploring how grounding strategies, breathwork, and visualization practices can fortify emotional presence and self-awareness.

Blending EMDR With Mindfulness

Integrating mindfulness practices with EMDR can significantly improve your sense of emotional awareness and presence, particularly for women like us—who are dealing with the aftermath of trauma. Mindfulness encourages us to connect deeply with the present moment, which can be incredibly beneficial during EMDR sessions where past traumas are processed. Mindful awareness techniques are essential tools in this integration process. These techniques, which include practices like mindful breathing and body scan meditations, help you anchor yourself in the here and now.

Grounding Techniques

Grounding strategies are a vital component of this integration. Techniques such as the 5-4-3-2-1 method allow you to engage your senses—sight, sound, touch, smell, and taste—to stay physically and emotionally rooted in the present (Raypole, 2024).

SIMPLE GROUNDING PRACTICE

For example, you can try this activity now, and then use the space below to reflect on how you felt before and after:

1. Take a deep breath and briefly note how you are feeling emotionally and physically.
2. Look around and name five things you can see.
3. Focus on four things you can touch and describe how they feel.
4. Identify three sounds you can hear.
5. Notice two scents around you (or recall a favorite smell).
6. Pay attention to one thing you can taste (sip a drink, chew gum, or just notice the taste in your mouth).
7. Take another deep breath and write a few sentences reflecting on how you feel now compared to before the exercise.

_____
_____
_____
_____
_____
_____

CATEGORY NAMING

Another grounding technique that you can use for this is called category naming, which helps pull your mind away from anxious thoughts and toward more intentional, logical lines of thinking. It seems like a simple activity, but when you use it often, it can help you calm and clear the mind in moments of distress. Here's how you'll do it:

1. Pause for a moment and take a deep breath.
2. Briefly note how you feel emotionally and physically.
3. Choose a category (e.g., animals, colors, fruits, cities, or book titles).

4. Name as many items in that category as you can in 30–60 seconds.
5. If your mind wanders, gently bring your focus back to the activity.
6. Take another deep breath and reflect on how you feel now compared to before.

_____
_____
_____
_____
_____
_____

TEXTURED OBJECT EXPLORATION

Engaging with texture can bring your awareness to the present moment and help regulate your nervous system. This activity guides you through a simple exploration you can use before or after EMDR to settle any distressing or anxious thoughts you may face:

1. Choose a textured object nearby (a piece of fabric, a stone, a leaf, or any small item with an interesting surface).
2. Hold the object and close your eyes. Slowly run your fingers over it, paying attention to its texture, temperature, and shape.
3. Describe the sensations to yourself in your mind (e.g., "smooth and cool," "rough with ridges").
4. Take slow, deep breaths as you explore. If intrusive thoughts arise, gently return your focus to the object.
5. After a minute or two, reflect on whether you feel more present and grounded.

SENSORY COUNTDOWN WALK

This activity combines grounding with movement, helping to release tension while staying present:

1. Take a short walk, either indoors or outside. As you walk, notice your surroundings through your senses:
    a. Identify 5 colors around you.
    b. Listen for 4 different sounds.
    c. Find 3 textures to touch.

      d. Notice 2 scents.

      e. Focus on 1 deep breath in and out.

2. Take a moment to reflect: Has your mind shifted from distress to presence? Do you feel calmer?

Grounding techniques make it easier to feel anchored in the present moment, especially when distressing emotions come into play. You can use grounding techniques on their own, or combine them with methods like breathwork to elevate their efficacy. And speaking of breathwork, let's explore that now!

Breathwork

Breathwork techniques can aid in calming the nervous system, which can lead to focus and reduce distractions.

DEEP BELLY BREATHING

Simple exercises like deep belly breathing encourage the activation of the body's relaxation response. You can perform deep belly breathing like so:

1. Sit or lie down in a quiet, comfortable space. Place one hand on your chest and the other on your belly.
2. Breathe in slowly through your nose for a count of four. Focus on expanding your belly rather than your chest.
3. Pause and hold your breath for a count of two.
4. Exhale through your mouth for a count of six, feeling your belly deflate. Imagine releasing tension with each breath out.
5. Continue for 5–10 rounds, maintaining a slow, controlled pace.
6. Notice any shifts in your body, emotions, or mental clarity. Ask yourself: *Do I feel more centered? Has my tension decreased?*

4-7-8 BREATHING

Another breathwork exercise you can use—one of my favorites—is called 4-7-8 breathing, and it works like this:

1. Sit or lie down in a relaxed position. Place the tip of your tongue against the roof of your mouth, just behind your front teeth.
2. Breathe in through your nose for a slow count of four, filling your belly with air.
3. Hold your breath for a count of seven while keeping your body relaxed.
4. Exhale completely through your mouth for a count of eight, making a gentle whooshing sound.
5. Complete four rounds of this breathing pattern. If needed, work up to eight cycles over time.

BOX BREATHING WITH HAND MOVEMENT

This exercise pairs controlled breathing with a physical anchor to deepen focus during EMDR practices or while preparing for them:

1. Extend one hand in front of you.
2. With your other hand, use a finger to trace a square in the air or along your palm as you breathe:
    a. Inhale for 4 seconds as you trace one side.
    b. Hold for 4 seconds as you trace the next.
    c. Exhale for 4 seconds, tracing the third side.
    d. Hold for 4 seconds, tracing the last side.
3. Repeat this cycle for a few rounds, noticing the calming effect on your body.

SIGHING BREATH RELEASE

This simple breathwork technique uses an audible sigh to release tension.

1. Take a deep inhale through your nose, filling your lungs completely.
2. Exhale through your mouth with an audible sigh, letting go of any tension.
3. Repeat 3–5 times, allowing each exhale to feel more natural and releasing.
4. Reflect on whether your body feels lighter or more relaxed afterward.

As with grounding, breathwork techniques are great on their own or paired with other practices, such as visualization. Let's talk about how visualization can help with reframing.

Visualization

Visualization practices, particularly those that work with positive imagery, play a significant role in empowering you before you get into trauma processing. Visualization involves creating mental images of soothing or uplifting scenes, which can build inner strength and resilience.

VISUALIZING A SAFE SPACE

Before an EMDR session, visualizing a safe place or possibly imagining oneself surrounded by supportive elements can bolster confidence and emotional preparedness (*Ascension Counseling, Ltd.*, 2024). With these steps, you can visualize an inner safe space that helps you feel stable and calm before or after EMDR:

1. Sit or lie down comfortably in a quiet area where you can relax without interruptions. Close your eyes and take a few deep breaths, bringing your attention to the present moment.
2. Picture a place where you feel completely safe, peaceful, and at ease. This could be a real location or a place of your own design. It could be a beach, forest, room, or even a cozy corner in your mind.
3. Engage your senses. What do you see, hear, smell, or feel in this space? Focus on the details, allowing yourself to immerse fully.
4. As you imagine your safe space, introduce supportive elements that bring you comfort, such as:
    a. Soft lighting or warmth.
    b. A protective figure or energy surrounding you.
    c. A peaceful sound, like birds chirping or waves crashing.
    d. A feeling of weightlessness or being wrapped in a soft embrace.
5. Allow yourself to fully experience the calm, comfort, and safety that this space provides. Visualize yourself becoming stronger and more resilient as you sit or move within this safe environment.
6. Take a few deep, grounding breaths, feeling the safety of this space fill your body and mind. Reflect on how you feel now compared to before starting the visualization. Are you more grounded, confident, or calm?
7. Before you finish, choose an anchor—a word, image, or gesture—that you can use in the future to evoke this safe space quickly. This could be a simple word like "peace," touching your fingers together, or visualizing a specific element of the space.

PROTECTIVE LIGHT VISUALIZATION

EMDR practices are inherently very vulnerable. You're exploring a lot of deep-seated experiences and traumas, and it can sometimes feel easier to engage with such practices when you feel protected. This protective light visualization can help you achieve just that by following these steps:

1. Close your eyes and take slow, steady breaths. Imagine a warm, glowing light hovering above you.

2. Picture this light slowly descending, surrounding your body with warmth, comfort, and safety.
3. Let the light act as a protective barrier, shielding you from distressing thoughts or emotions.
4. If you encounter any negative energy, visualize the light dissolving it gently and replacing it with peace.
5. Stay with this imagery for a few moments, then take a deep breath and return to the present feeling safe and grounded.

It's important to recognize that these mindfulness practices do not stand alone but rather complement and enhance the effectiveness of EMDR therapy. When you learn to apply these techniques consistently, you'll likely find an increase in your overall emotional resilience and capacity for self-soothing.

Connecting Past And Present

Facilitating the connection between past traumas and present-day healing through EMDR is central to understanding how you can move forward in your recovery journey. A key concept in trauma healing is temporal awareness, which involves acknowledging how past experiences shape current thoughts and behaviors. Trauma often leaves lasting impressions that influence how we respond to present situations. Being aware of this can empower us to identify patterns and make more conscious choices moving forward. For example, a person who experienced neglect in childhood might unconsciously seek validation from others as an adult. This behavior stems from past unmet needs and can manifest in various aspects of their life, including relationships and self-perception.

Mapping traumatic events is a practical method to visually represent timelines of emotional responses and connect past experiences to present-day ones through temporal awareness. This technique can be particularly beneficial for anyone struggling to articulate complex feelings associated with past trauma. If you're interested in giving this a try, here's an activity that can help:

1. Draw a horizontal line across a page, marking it with labels for key years or periods in your life (e.g., childhood, early adulthood, recent years).

2. Mark significant traumatic events on the timeline. These could be related to family, relationships, loss, or personal challenges.
3. For each event, write down how you felt at the time and what emotional responses still linger today. Use colors, symbols, or brief phrases to make these connections more visual.
4. Look for patterns in your emotional responses. Do certain triggers or events still have a strong emotional pull today? Are there patterns of reaction that you'd like to explore or shift?
5. Take a moment to reflect by pondering the insights you've gained from mapping these connections. Consider how you might use this map in future therapy sessions or as a tool for processing emotions.

Moving Forward

In this chapter, we've explored how blending EMDR with mindfulness can be a game-changer for healing. These practices, like mindful breathing and grounding exercises, give you the tools to stay present and calm when facing past traumas. Whether you're working through trauma yourself or supporting others, these practices encourage a more profound connection to oneself and the community. Integrating mindfulness with EMDR offers a holistic path forward, creating space for healing that builds strength and renews hope.

Chapter Four

PRACTICAL EMDR EXERCISES FOR DAILY LIFE

Incorporating EMDR exercises into daily life can be an incredible experience as you walk the path of trauma recovery. These practices are designed to extend beyond traditional therapy sessions and offer a way to integrate healing into everyday routines, which makes recovery feel more natural and less daunting. When applied consistently outside of professional settings, these exercises can be powerful methods to help manage stress, enhance resilience, and create a sense of control over your mental health journey.

Creating A Daily EMDR Routine

Establishing a structured routine that incorporates EMDR principles can be an efficacious tool in enhancing trauma recovery. The key to this approach is consistency, which plays a major role in helping you develop habits of self-care and emotional regulation. Regular practice of EMDR exercises helps the mind and body become accustomed to constructive coping mechanisms.

Consistency doesn't mean rigidity, though. It means creating a rhythm that fits into your life seamlessly and offers a stable foundation upon which healing can occur. For example, knowing you have designated times for EMDR exercises each day can provide reassurance and structure. This regularity can activate a calming response, as it lets the nervous system relax with the assurance that there is a predictable pattern to follow.

Morning And Evening Routines

Morning and evening are ideal anchors for these routines. Starting your day with EMDR exercises can set a positive tone and mentally prepare you for whatever the day might bring. A simple morning routine could involve a few minutes of mindfulness meditation combined with bilateral stimulation, such as tapping your knees alternately. This centers your thoughts and aligns your physical state with emotional equilibrium (*Ascension Counseling, Ltd.*, 2024). Similarly, winding down with a short EMDR practice in the evening can promote better sleep by clearing the mind of the day's residual stresses.

Creating a routine of your own can seem daunting, but you're not without direction in doing so. With this activity, you can create a morning or evening routine that integrates EMDR while fitting perfectly within your lifestyle:

1. Decide if you want to create a morning routine, a night routine, or both.
2. Select grounding practices that you want to incorporate. If you're not sure which options might be best, you can use these examples:
   a. For Morning:
      i. Mindfulness Meditation: Spend 3–5 minutes practicing mindfulness by focusing on your breath, bringing your attention back to the present moment whenever your mind wanders.
      ii. Bilateral Stimulation: While sitting comfortably, tap your knees alternately (right-left-right) for 2–3 minutes. Focus on the sensation of the tapping, allowing it to calm and center you.

   b. For Night:
      i. Deep Breathing: Practice 4-7-8 breathing for 5 minutes before bed.
      ii. Gentle EMDR Practice: Sit quietly and use bilateral stimulation (e.g., tapping your knees) while recalling neutral or positive memories to clear the mind of residual stress.
3. Write down the specific steps of your chosen routine (e.g., "In the morning, I will sit quietly, breathe deeply, and tap my knees for 3 minutes").

_____
_____
_____
_____

4. Set a specific time frame for your routine: How long will you dedicate to each practice?

   _____
   _____
   _____
   _____

5. Add any elements that make your routine feel calming or empowering (e.g., soft music, a calming essential oil, or a comforting beverage).
6. Commit to trying your routine for at least one week. Mark your calendar or set a reminder to help make this a consistent part of your day.
7. After one week, write down any changes you notice:

   a. How do you feel after your morning routine?

   _____
   _____
   _____
   _____

   b. How did the night routine affect your sleep?

   _____
   _____
   _____
   _____

   c. Would you adjust any part of the routine?

   _____
   _____
   _____
   _____

Adding EMDR To Daily Activities

Integrating EMDR practices into daily activities can also make healing feel more natural and less like a chore. Think about incorporating bilateral stimulation during everyday tasks, like listening to binaural beats while on a walk or doing gentle shoulder taps while cooking. These small adjustments can create moments of mindfulness throughout your day, allowing you to manage anxiety or stress efficiently. The key is to align these practices with activities you already engage in to make them a seamless part of your life rather than additional burdens.

It's important to remember that while having a routine is beneficial, flexibility within that routine is equally essential. Personal growth isn't linear; it requires adapting your practices as you evolve. There might be days when sticking to your regular schedule feels impossible due to life's demands. On such occasions, give yourself the grace to adjust without guilt. The goal is progress, not perfection. Be open to changing your approach if certain practices are no longer serving you effectively.

Visual And Sensory Techniques

Utilizing visual and sensory tools can greatly enhance the effectiveness of EMDR exercises in everyday life. This practice leverages our inherent sensory perceptions to harness emotional healing.

Imagery And Safe Spaces

Creating mental images of secure and comforting environments can provide a refuge during overwhelming moments. For example, picturing a serene beach where the gentle waves lap against the shore can help transport your mind to a place of tranquility. When stress strikes, these mental retreats ground the mind.

Tactile Engagement

Engaging with objects that have various textures can be incredibly grounding. No matter if it's the cool smoothness of a polished stone or the soft comfort of a plush fabric, touching these items can redirect focus and help channel emotional energy more constructively. Tactile experiences are direct and immediate; they provide a sensory reality check that can help dissipate anxiety. For example, carrying a piece of velvet or a worry stone in your pocket can serve as a physical reminder of stability and grounding.

During moments of stress, simply reaching out to touch these objects can provide a calming effect, helping to center emotions and thoughts.

It might not be immediately apparent how tactile engagement can make a real difference in your emotional levels, especially when it comes to reducing anxiety. However, when put into use, tactile engagement can have incredible benefits. Give this activity a try to see them for yourself, and don't be afraid to revisit this activity whenever you'd like:

1. Select an object that has a texture you find soothing or interesting. This could be something you already own, like a velvet cloth or a polished stone, or you could go out and find something new that feels comforting to touch.
2. Sit in a quiet space and hold the object in your hand. Close your eyes and focus entirely on the sensation of the object. Notice its texture—how does it feel on your skin? Is it soft, smooth, bumpy, or cool? Run your fingers over the surface, exploring every detail of its texture. Let the sensation anchor your awareness to the present moment.
3. As you hold or touch the object, take slow, deep breaths. With each inhale, feel your body relax, and with each exhale, release any tension or stress you are holding. Focus on the grounding nature of the object. Imagine it is a physical reminder of stability and emotional calm.
4. Keep the object nearby, whether in your pocket or in a place where you can easily reach it. When you begin to feel overwhelmed, anxious, or stressed, take a moment to touch or hold the object. Focus on its texture and allow it to re-center your thoughts and emotions.
5. After using the object, take a moment to reflect on the experience in your journal:
    a. How did touching the object affect my emotions?

    _____
    _____
    _____

    b. Did I notice any physical sensations of relaxation or grounding?

    _____
    _____
    _____

    c. How can I incorporate this grounding technique into my routine?

_____
_____
_____

Combining Tools

Finally, by blending these sensory elements, multisensory experiences can be even more effective. Combining visual, tactile, and auditory components enriches the overall EMDR experience by making it more engaging and holistic. A practical guideline for creating multisensory experiences involves experimenting with different combinations of sensory stimuli to discover which works best for the individual. Try layering these elements gradually, starting with one sensory tool before incorporating others, to find the most comforting blend.

Tracking Progress And Changes

Monitoring progress is a necessary aspect of healing, especially when engaging in EMDR-based exercises outside therapy sessions. Keeping track of your growth means that you can validate your journey and identify areas that might need more attention.

Journaling

One effective way to monitor progress is through journaling techniques. Journaling allows you to capture your thoughts, feelings, and responses on paper, providing a clearer picture of your emotional journey. Expressive writing, a popular technique, involves delving into your deepest thoughts for a few moments each session. This process can uncover patterns or repeated themes that may need work. For example, you can use these journal prompts—and the space below—to engage in expressive writing:

- Describe a recent moment where I felt overwhelmed or triggered. What was happening at that time? How did I react emotionally, and what thoughts accompanied those feelings? What would I want to change or do differently next time?

- What patterns or themes have I noticed in my emotional responses over the past few weeks? Are there moments when I feel stronger or more at peace? How can I nurture these strengths moving forward?
- Think about where I was emotionally a month ago. What has changed since then? What new coping strategies or insights have I gained? How can I continue to build on these positive changes?
- Who or what makes me feel safe and supported during difficult moments? Describe how these people or things help me in my healing process. What do I need from my support system that I haven't yet asked for?
- What is one fear I have about my healing process? What does that fear look like, and how does it affect me? How can I work to face or release this fear?
- Write a letter to my past self, acknowledging the pain and struggles, but also celebrating the resilience and growth. What does my past self need to hear from me right now?
- Imagine myself one year from now, having healed and grown. What do I look like? How do I feel? What lessons have I learned that I can carry with me into the future?

Also, gratitude journaling helps maintain focus on positive aspects, which can be incredibly uplifting during difficult times (Miller, 2019). Here's a simple gratitude journaling exercise you can engage with to achieve this:

1. List three things you are grateful for today. These can be big or small—anything that brings you a sense of appreciation or joy.

2. Reflect on why each of these things brings you gratitude. How do they make you feel? Why are they meaningful to you?

3. Write about one positive experience from today, no matter how small. What made it stand out and why does it bring you peace or happiness?

4. Identify one thing you're looking forward to. This could be an event, a goal, or something simple like a quiet moment.

5. End your journaling with a sentence or two of affirmation: "*I am grateful for the strength I am cultivating in this moment.*"

Developing Metrics

Developing metrics for success is another helpful element. Setting personal benchmarks provides a framework to measure your progress against. Think of these as little milestones on your healing journey. They don't have to be complex; simple goals like feeling calm for an hour after practicing an EMDR exercise or sleeping better after a week can serve as indicators. Establish measurable outcomes, such as reduced anxiety or improved sleep quality, to help gauge improvement over time. If you're unsure of where to start when it comes to setting up simple metrics, give this activity a try:

1. Reflect on the areas you want to track and improve. These could include anxiety levels, sleep quality, emotional stability, or physical relaxation. Choose 1–3 areas that are most relevant to your current healing process.

   _____
   _____
   _____
   _____

2. For each area, establish a specific, measurable goal. These goals should be small enough to be achievable but significant enough to show progress.

   _____
   _____
   _____
   _____

3. Set a timeframe for achieving each goal. This could be daily, weekly, or monthly—depending on the goal's nature.

   _____
   _____
   _____
   _____

4. Use a simple journal or chart to track your progress. For example, you could mark a "calm" day or note any improvements in sleep quality. For each goal, write a quick note on how you felt or any changes you noticed.

   _____
   _____
   _____
   _____

5. At the end of your established timeframe, review your results. Celebrate small successes and identify areas for improvement. Adjust your goals if necessary to continue your growth.

   _____
   _____
   _____
   _____

Moving Forward

Taking what we've covered about integrating EMDR practices into everyday life, it's clear that creating a personal routine can be a game-changer. Making these exercises part of your regular schedule means that you are giving yourself the gift of stability and support, fitting them in when it makes sense for you—whether that's tapping out stress before bed or setting a calm tone in the morning. This kind of consistency turns self-care from a chore into a natural part of your day, helping you manage emotions better and build resilience over time.

Chapter Five

LONG-TERM EMDR HEALING

EMDR is a long-term tool for healing and resilience. Integrating it into your ongoing recovery means that you can systematically reprocess traumatic memories while developing strategies to maintain progress. This chapter provides two key activities: one to help you create a comprehensive EMDR plan tailored to your recovery and another for tracking progress over time.

Activity 1: Developing Your Personalized EMDR Plan

To make EMDR an effective long-term tool, it's important to create a structured but flexible plan that accounts for your unique trauma history, emotional capacity, and personal goals. This activity will guide you through crafting an individualized EMDR plan for your healing journey.

Step 1: Identify Your Core Trauma Themes

List recurring themes or patterns in your traumatic memories. These may include feelings of abandonment, powerlessness, or shame. Group similar experiences together under these themes.

Step 2: Assess Your Readiness For Processing

Using a scale of 1-10 (1 being completely overwhelmed, 10 being highly prepared), rate your emotional readiness to address each theme. Start with those rated 6 or above, as they may be more accessible for reprocessing without overwhelming distress.

Step 3: Define Your Healing Goals

For each trauma theme, write down what healing would look like. For example:
- **Theme:** Fear of rejection
- **Healing Goal:** Feel secure in my relationships without fearing abandonment

Step 4: Select Your Target Memories

Within each theme, choose specific memories that strongly represent your trauma. These will be the targets for EMDR processing. Write them down in order of emotional intensity, starting with moderately distressing memories before tackling the most severe ones.

_____
_____
_____
_____
_____
_____

Step 5: Identify Positive Cognitions

For each target memory, replace the negative belief you hold with a positive one. Examples include:

- Negative Belief: *"I am unworthy of love."*
- Positive Cognition: *"I am deserving of love and respect."*

_____
_____
_____
_____
_____
_____

Step 6: Establish Coping Strategies

Before engaging in EMDR processing, ensure you have self-soothing techniques to manage emotional distress. These may include grounding exercises, safe place visualization, or somatic practices. Write your techniques down below.

_____
_____
_____
_____

Step 7: Determine Your EMDR Frequency

Decide how often you will engage in EMDR processing, whether through self-guided techniques (if working independently) or structured sessions with a therapist. Set realistic expectations based on your capacity.

Step 8: Create A Support System

Healing is not meant to be done in isolation. Identify friends, family members, or support groups that you can lean on when needed. Also, note any professional support available, such as an EMDR-trained therapist.

Activity 2: Tracking Your EMDR Progress

Maintaining a record of your EMDR work helps reinforce healing and offers insight into patterns of progress. This activity provides a structured method to track your recovery journey over time.

Step 1: Create An EMDR Progress Journal

Dedicate a notebook or digital document specifically for tracking your EMDR sessions and their effects.

Step 2: Record Each Session's Key Details

For each EMDR session (self-guided or therapist-led), record:

Date of session _____

Target memory processed _____

Initial distress level (0-10 scale) _____

Negative belief before processing _____

Positive belief after processing _____

Final distress level (0-10 scale) _____

Physical or emotional sensations experienced: _____
_____

Step 3: Note Post-Session Effects

After each session, track any emotional shifts, triggers, or insights that arise in the days following. Here are some questions to reflect on:

- Did you notice changes in how you think about the memory?
- Were there any unexpected emotions or bodily sensations?
- Did you experience relief, clarity, or resistance?

Step 4: Identify Patterns Over Time

Every few weeks, review your journal and look for trends:

- Are distress levels decreasing over time?
- Are certain memories still triggering, indicating more work is needed?
- Have your emotional reactions or self-beliefs shifted positively?

Step 5: Adjust Your Approach As Needed

Healing is non-linear, so adjust your EMDR plan based on what your tracking reveals. If certain memories remain highly distressing, consider revisiting coping strategies before reprocessing further.

Step 6: Celebrate Milestones

Acknowledge and celebrate progress, no matter how small. Recognizing improvements reinforces the effectiveness of EMDR and motivates continued healing.

WRITING SPACE

If you would prefer to keep your log in this workbook, you can use this space for your tracking:

_____
_____
_____
_____
_____
_____
_____
_____
_____
_____
_____
_____
_____
_____
_____
_____
_____
_____
_____
_____

Activity 3: Creating An Emotional Regulation Toolkit

While EMDR helps process trauma, ongoing emotional regulation is necessary for managing distress between sessions. This activity will guide you in assembling a personalized toolkit of strategies to navigate emotional ups and downs.

Step 1: Identify Your Common Emotional Triggers

List situations, thoughts, or interactions that frequently cause distress. Examples can include:

- Conflict with loved ones
- Feeling misunderstood
- Unexpected reminders of trauma

Step 2: Select Regulation Techniques For Each Trigger

For each trigger you identified, choose at least one strategy from different categories:
- Cognitive (Reframing negative thoughts, using affirmations)
- Somatic (Breathing exercises, movement-based grounding)
- Sensory (Holding a comforting object, listening to music)
- Social (Calling a trusted friend, engaging in a safe online support space)

_____
_____
_____
_____
_____
_____

Step 3: Create A Physical Or Digital Toolkit

Write your strategies on note cards, in a journal, or as a phone note for easy access. Consider assembling physical items (like a grounding stone or essential oil) in a small box.

_____
_____
_____
_____
_____
_____

Step 4: Practice Using Your Toolkit Proactively

Use your techniques regularly, not just during distress. This strengthens your ability to regulate emotions instinctively.

Activity 4: Processing EMDR Insights Through Expressive Writing

EMDR often brings up deep insights and emotions that may not be fully verbalized during sessions. This activity helps you integrate those experiences through structured writing.

Step 1: Choose A Prompt

After an EMDR session, write about one of the following:
- What did I learn about myself from today's session?
- How do I feel differently about the memory I processed?
- What unexpected emotions surfaced, and what might they mean?

_____
_____
_____
_____
_____
_____
_____
_____
_____

Step 2: Write Freely And Without Judgment

Set a timer for 10–15 minutes and write without stopping or editing. Let emotions flow naturally.

_____
_____
_____
_____
_____
_____
_____
_____
_____
_____

Step 3: Reflect On Your Writing

Afterward, underline any words or phrases that stand out. What patterns or shifts do you notice?

_____
_____
_____
_____
_____
_____
_____
_____
_____

Step 4: Decide On A Next Step

Based on your reflection, identify an action and engage with it based on your insights gained in this activity:

- Reaffirm a new belief, such as *"I am safe now."*
- Discuss a realization with a therapist or trusted person.
- Create an affirmation based on your writing.

_____
_____
_____
_____
_____
_____
_____
_____
_____
_____
_____

Activity 5: Grounding Through Rituals And

Routine

Reprocessing trauma can be destabilizing, so grounding yourself in meaningful routines creates a sense of safety and predictability. This activity will help you design small rituals to anchor yourself.

Step 1: Identify Areas That Need Stability

Reflect on aspects of daily life where grounding would help, such as:
- Morning or evening routines (starting or ending the day with calm)
- After EMDR sessions (transitioning out of processing mode)
- During stressful moments (having a centering practice to return to)

Step 2: Choose Simple, Intentional Practices

Select small, repeatable actions that feel comforting. Examples might include:
- Drinking a warm cup of tea before bed
- Lighting a candle and setting an intention for the day
- Taking a mindful walk after an EMDR session
- Running your hands under cold water when feeling overwhelmed

---

Step 3: Commit to Your Rituals

Write down when and how you'll use your chosen practices. Consistency helps reinforce a sense of security.

Moving Forward

Developing a structured EMDR plan and tracking your progress helps you integrate this incredible therapy into your long-term recovery. Healing from C-PTSD is something that unfolds at its own pace, but with intentionality and commitment, EMDR can become a lasting resource for reclaiming your life.

Conclusion

Healing from complex PTSD is a journey of self-discovery, resilience, and growth. Throughout this book, we have explored the profound impact of EMDR therapy, from its foundational principles to practical exercises that empower you to engage with your healing in a meaningful way. We've also examined how EMDR can be integrated with mindfulness, somatic practices, and other therapeutic modalities to create a holistic approach to trauma recovery.

One of the most important takeaways from this journey is that healing is not a linear process. On some days, progress may feel tangible and incredible, while on others, you may encounter resistance or resurfacing trauma responses. This is natural. EMDR, when used consistently and with intention, provides a powerful method for gently unraveling the layers of past wounds, reframing negative beliefs, and restoring a sense of emotional balance.

As you continue integrating EMDR into your daily life, consider these key practices to support your healing:

- **Commit to Small, Sustainable Steps**: Healing does not require perfection; it requires consistency. Whether through guided bilateral stimulation, journaling, or mindfulness exercises, find small ways to incorporate EMDR techniques into your routine.
- **Honor Your Nervous System's Needs**: Some days, EMDR practices may feel overwhelming, and that's okay. Learning to listen to your body's signals and adjusting your approach accordingly will ensure that your healing remains supportive rather than triggering.

- **Combine EMDR With Grounding and Self-Compassion Practices:** Mindfulness, breathwork, and similar exercises can enhance the benefits of EMDR by reinforcing a sense of safety and presence in your body. Self-compassion is also vital—be kind to yourself as you navigate emotional processing.
- **Recognize Your Growth:** Reflecting on how far you've come is just as important as identifying what still needs healing. Even the smallest shifts in perspective, emotional regulation, or resilience are significant markers of progress.
- **Seek Support When Needed:** Healing is deeply personal, but it doesn't have to be done alone. Whether working with an EMDR therapist, engaging in support groups, or leaning on trusted loved ones, allowing yourself to receive support can accelerate and deepen your recovery.

Remember, EMDR is not just about processing past trauma—it's about reclaiming your present and building a future where you feel safe, empowered, and whole. As you move forward, trust in your capacity to heal, and know that each step you take is an act of profound self-love and resilience. Your past does not define you, but how you choose to heal from it will shape the life you create for yourself.

You are worthy of peace, healing, and joy. Let EMDR be a guiding light on your path to reclaiming all that you deserve.

Book Five

PAVING A BETTER LIFE THROUGH RESILIENCE AND MINDFULNESS

Introduction

Healing from complex PTSD is not just a matter of processing the past—it revolves around building a future where resilience becomes second nature. This final book in the series is dedicated to helping you cultivate lasting strength, emotional balance, and self-trust.

The focus here is on long-term empowerment, driving you to take control of your life and grow into the best version of yourself without C-PTSD holding you back.

Resilience is not an inherent trait but a skill that can be developed through daily habits, mindset shifts, and intentional self-care practices. Exploring how mindfulness and neuroplasticity can reshape your inner narrative, how to hone resilience, and more means that you'll learn how to reshape the patterns that trauma has left behind. This book will also guide you in creating a Personal Resilience Action Plan, ensuring that your healing journey continues beyond structured therapy sessions and becomes an integral part of your everyday life.

This is your opportunity to step forward with confidence, equipped with the tools to navigate life's challenges from a place of strength, self-awareness, and emotional stability. Remember, healing is not just about surviving—it's about thriving. Let's begin.

Chapter One

UNDERSTANDING RESILIENCE—THE KEY TO OVERCOMING TRAUMA

Resilience is all about bouncing back from the tough stuff life throws at us. It's a bit like having a personal superpower that helps you handle things when they get difficult. But what makes someone resilient, especially when dealing with the aftermath of trauma? This chapter dives into this subject to show you how certain traits can help people recover and thrive, even after experiencing significant challenges.

Characteristics Of Resilient People

When it comes to bouncing back from life's challenges, resilient people possess certain traits that enable them to navigate adversity with strength and optimism. Understanding these traits can be empowering, helping you to recognize your own strengths and foster resilience in your life.

Adaptability

One of the standout characteristics of resilient people is adaptability. They possess a unique ability to roll with the punches and adapt to changing circumstances without losing their footing. When faced with unexpected challenges, resilient individuals look for ways to adjust their plans rather than being paralyzed by uncertainty or fear. This flexibility helps them remain focused on their goals despite the chaos around them, maintaining a sense of stability and purpose.

The good news is that adaptability is something you can cultivate through practice and conscious effort. While adaptability can take some time to gain as a skill, activities like this one can make picking up an adaptable mindset easier:

1. **Reflect on Past Adaptability:** Think of a time when something didn't go as planned. How did you react? What emotions surfaced? Looking back, what could you have done differently to adapt more smoothly?

   _____
   _____
   _____

2. **Reframe a Current Challenge:** Identify a current situation where you feel stuck or frustrated. Write down the specific obstacle and why it feels difficult.

   _____
   _____
   _____

   a. Now, list at least three alternative ways to approach or adjust to the situation.

   _____
   _____
   _____

3. **Practice "What If?" Thinking:** Choose a common scenario that causes you stress (e.g., plans falling through, unexpected work changes).

   a. Ask yourself: What if this happens? How can I respond in a way that keeps me calm and focused?

   _____
   _____
   _____
   _____

   b. Write down a flexible response plan for each scenario to train your mind in adaptable thinking.

_____
_____
_____

4. **Adopt a Growth Statement:** Create a personal affirmation to remind yourself that change is manageable. Repeat this affirmation whenever you feel resistance to change.

    _____
    _____
    _____

5. **Reflect:** After completing the activity, note any shifts in perspective. Did exploring alternative solutions help reduce frustration? How did creating a plan for adaptability change your mindset about uncertainty? Over time, practicing this exercise can help build the resilience needed to embrace change rather than fear it.

    _____
    _____
    _____

Optimism

Optimism is another trait commonly found in resilient people. It involves maintaining a hopeful outlook even when things get tough. Optimism doesn't mean ignoring reality; instead, it means recognizing difficulties while believing in the possibility of positive outcomes. Resilient people are often able to find the silver lining in challenging situations, which helps them cope better and recover more quickly from setbacks. For example, when my friend Alexa encounters a difficult situation, she looks at it as something she can use to grow. Instead of ignoring the negatives, she considers them carefully—especially what she can learn from them and how they help her. This means tricky situations don't affect her as severely as they might for someone without resilience.

Being optimistic can feel challenging, but simple daily habits can help elevate your sense of optimism. Slowly, these habits will help you grow and face challenges with greater resilience. To get started with this, pick one of the following daily habits and commit to it for a week. Then, reflect on how that habit improved your sense of optimism.

- **Gratitude Journaling:** Write down three things you are grateful for each day.

- **Positive Affirmations:** Start your morning with powerful, uplifting statements.
- **Acts of Kindness:** Do one small kind act for someone else.
- **Mindful Breathing:** Take a few moments to focus on deep, calming breaths.
- **Reframing Negativity:** When a challenge arises, ask yourself: "*What can I learn from this?*"
- **Celebrate Small Wins:** Acknowledge even the tiniest achievements.
- **Limit Negative Input:** Reduce exposure to negativity (news, social media, or toxic conversations).

_____
_____
_____
_____
_____

Growth Mindset

Furthermore, a growth mindset is necessary for personal development and resilience. This perspective encourages seeing challenges as opportunities to learn and grow. Embracing a growth mindset means you're open to change, willing to learn from mistakes, and ready to take calculated risks that lead to improvement. Such an attitude leads to resilience because it shifts your focus from fearing failure to valuing the lessons learned along the way. To help you begin working with a growth mindset, give this activity a try:

1. Choose one small task outside your comfort zone (e.g., trying a new hobby, speaking up in a group, or changing a daily routine).
2. Instead of thinking, "*I might fail,*" reframe it as, "*This is an opportunity to learn and grow.*"
3. Complete the task, focusing on effort rather than perfection.
4. Write down one thing you learned or accomplished, no matter how small.

_____
_____
_____

Emotional Intelligence

Resilient individuals also demonstrate high emotional intelligence, which plays a big role in managing stress and adversity. Being attuned to your emotions means that you can understand what's causing them and respond appropriately. Emotional regulation—another key aspect of emotional intelligence—helps you stay calm under pressure, avoiding knee-jerk reactions that might worsen a situation.

EMOTIONAL INTELLIGENCE SELF-ASSESSMENT

Answer each question honestly on a scale from 1 to 5 (1 = Never, 5 = Always). Then, review your lowest-scoring area to identify a focus for improvement.

- Self-Awareness
    - I can easily identify what I'm feeling and why.
    - I recognize how my emotions influence my thoughts and behaviors.
    - I take time to reflect on my emotional responses rather than reacting immediately.
- Emotional Regulation
    - I stay calm and collected in stressful situations.
    - I can shift my mindset when negative emotions arise.
    - I avoid letting frustration or anger control my actions.
- Empathy & Social Awareness
    - I can sense how others are feeling, even if they don't say it outright.
    - I listen actively and try to understand different perspectives.
    - I adjust my communication based on the emotional state of others.
- Relationship Management
    - I handle conflicts in a constructive and respectful way.
    - I express my emotions clearly and effectively in relationships.
    - I support others emotionally without feeling overwhelmed myself.

REFLECTION:

- Which section had the lowest average score?
- What's one step you can take this week to improve in that area?
- How might strengthening this aspect of emotional intelligence help you build resilience?

Building Optimism And Hope

Optimism and hope can be incredibly beneficial during trauma recovery. These qualities help us reframe experiences and envision a brighter future. Let's discuss how various techniques can nurture both hope and optimism while guiding the journey toward healing.

Visualization Techniques

Visualization techniques are wonderful for strengthening optimism. It involves actively picturing yourself attaining personal goals or overcoming challenges. Visualization isn't just imagining success but feeling it—envisioning the relief, joy, and satisfaction accompanying those positive results. If you're interested in working to strengthen optimism by mentally experiencing success and the emotions that come with it, try out this visualization exercise:

1. Sit comfortably and close your eyes. Take a few deep breaths to relax.
2. Imagine yourself achieving a personal goal or overcoming a challenge. What does the scene look like? Where are you? Who is with you?
3. Hear the sounds around you—congratulatory words, laughter, or peaceful silence.
4. Feel the emotions—pride, relief, joy.
5. Notice any physical sensations—warmth, lightness, or energy.
6. Take a deep breath and mentally affirm: "*I am capable of achieving my goals.*" Hold onto the positive emotions as you return to the present.

Affirmations And Positive Self-Talk

Affirmations and positive self-talk are other important components of establishing hope in your mental outlook. They assist in cultivating a strong sense of self-worth while counteracting negative thoughts. Regularly affirming your strengths and capabilities can shift your focus away from what went wrong in the past towards what can go right in the future. Chances are, you deal with some thoughts that aren't positive—known as negative self-talk. One of the simplest ways to begin working with positive self-talk is by reframing those thoughts through activities like this one:

1. **Identify a Negative Thought:** Write down a self-critical or discouraging thought you often have (e.g., "*I always mess things up.*").

   _____
   _____
   _____

2. **Challenge It:** Ask yourself—is this thought absolutely true? Would I say this to a loved one?

   _____
   _____
   _____

3. **Rewrite It Positively:** Transform it into a supportive statement (e.g., "*I make mistakes, but I also learn and grow from them.*").

   _____
   _____
   _____

4. **Practice & Repeat:** Say your new affirmation out loud or write it down daily.

   _____
   _____
   _____

5. **Reflection:** Notice how changing your self-talk affects your mood and confidence. What's one positive phrase you can remind yourself of each day?

   _____
   _____
   _____

Realistic Expectations

Setting realistic expectations is also necessary when it comes to balancing optimism with achievable goals. When recovering from trauma, it's easy to feel overwhelmed. Optimism doesn't mean ignoring difficulties; it means approaching them with practical strategies. Establishing attainable goals provides structure and direction that helps you track progress over time. This approach mitigates feelings of discouragement that might arise from setting unrealistic standards.

The Role Of Community And Professional Support

Community support is absolutely beneficial when it comes to building resilience, especially for women like you and I who have faced trauma. The healing journey can be challenging, but having strong connections with others significantly improves your ability to bounce back and recover emotionally.

Support groups are immensely helpful here. They offer a space where you can voice your fears, express your emotions without judgment, and explore coping strategies. For example, my friend who was navigating C-PTSD joined a support group where she found other women who've walked similar paths. Listening to their stories and sharing her own helped her gain a sense of solidarity and mutual empowerment.

While community bonds are invaluable, there are moments when professional help can be more effective. Seeking guidance from mental health professionals integrates expert intervention into the benefits of community support. Therapists, counselors, and psychologists bring specialized knowledge that can address specific trauma-related issues by offering tailored strategies for recovery.

When accessing professional help, it's necessary to approach it as a complement to existing support systems rather than a standalone solution. A therapist might work alongside support groups to develop personalized coping mechanisms or offer additional context on trauma's impact on your life. With that said, having goals and realistic expectations for therapy and professional help can ensure that your support is meeting your needs, and this activity can help you determine your goals:

1. **Identify Your Main Concern:** What specific issue or challenge do you want therapy to help with? (e.g., anxiety, trauma processing, emotional regulation)

   _____
   _____
   _____

2. **Set Three Therapy Goals:** Think about what progress looks like for you and write down some goals.

   a. Example goals:

   i. I want to feel more in control of my emotions during stressful situations.

   ii. I want to develop healthier coping mechanisms for triggers.

   iii. I want to improve my self-confidence and self-compassion.

   b. _____
   _____
   _____

3. **Consider Supportive Strategies:** How can therapy complement your other support systems (e.g., journaling, support groups, self-care routines)?

   _____
   _____
   _____

4. **Measure Progress:** How will you know you're making progress? Write one small sign of improvement to look for in the next month.

   _____
   _____
   _____
   _____

Moving Forward

As we wrap up this chapter on resilience, it's important to remember that adopting these traits can truly change the way you experience life's challenges. We've explored how adaptability, optimism, and a growth mindset are key in building resilience and established that these characteristics are not just inherent but can be learned and strengthened through practice.

Chapter Two

DAILY HABITS FOR EMOTIONAL HEALTH AND WELL-BEING

Establishing daily habits is an important part of maintaining emotional health and well-being. The decisions we make, from what to eat to when to sleep, play a big part in shaping our emotional landscape.

In this chapter, we're going to talk about how you can reinforce emotional health through practical daily routines. You'll discover how nutrition and sleep support your emotional well-being (helping you stay centered and resilient), the impact that food choices can have on your mood and mental clarity (emphasizing the benefits of nutrient-rich diets), and more to help you continue to grow as you heal from C-PTSD.

Nutrition And Sleep Importance

When it comes to maintaining emotional health, two key aspects are often underestimated: nutrition and sleep. These elements serve as the foundation for our mental well-being, yet they frequently go unnoticed in the hustle and bustle of daily life.

Nutrition

First, let's talk about nutrition. What we eat has a notable effect on how we feel mentally and emotionally. A balanced diet—rich in vitamins, minerals, and antioxidants—can significantly influence mood fluctuations and overall mental stability. When our bodies receive the nutrients they need, our brains function more efficiently and stably. Eating high-quality foods, such as fruits, vegetables, whole grains, lean proteins, and healthy fats, nourishes the brain and protects it from oxidative stress (Selhub, 2022). Making positive shifts in diet requires understanding your current habits, and you can work through the following to gain this awareness:

1. List everything you ate and drank yesterday.

   _____
   _____
   _____

2. Did you include:
    a. Fruits and vegetables? (Yes/No)
    b. Whole grains? (Yes/No)
    c. Lean protein sources? (Yes/No)
    d. Healthy fats (e.g., nuts, avocados, olive oil)? (Yes/No)

3. How do your eating habits affect your mood and energy levels? Do you notice any crashes, cravings, or emotional eating patterns?

   _____
   _____
   _____

4. Choose one simple change to improve your nutrition this week (e.g., "Add an extra serving of vegetables to lunch" or "Drink more water instead of sugary drinks").

   _____
   _____
   _____

Now, if you're wondering which specific foods to put on your grocery list, consider those high in omega-3 fatty acids. These are found in fish like salmon and sardines, as well as flaxseeds and walnuts. Omega-3s improve brain function by elevating mood, reducing anxiety, and contributing to the production of serotonin. Research indicates that these fats form an integral part of neuronal cell membranes—they regulate neurotransmission, protect neurons, and have anti-inflammatory properties (Lachance & Ramsey, 2015). Foods high in vitamins B and C, iron, and protein are also beneficial.

Making new nutritional habits can feel daunting. However, with a simple checklist like this one, you can begin identifying where changes should be made to improve your diet in line with your needs for C-PTSD recovery:

- **Balance Blood Sugar:** Eat regular, nutrient-dense meals to prevent energy crashes and mood swings.
- **Increase Protein Intake:** Supports neurotransmitter function and stabilizes mood.
- **Incorporate Healthy Fats:** Omega-3s (found in fish, flaxseeds, and walnuts) reduce inflammation and support brain health.
- **Prioritize Whole Foods:** Minimize processed foods and focus on whole grains, lean proteins, fruits, and vegetables.
- **Hydration Check:** Drink enough water daily to maintain focus and reduce fatigue.
- **Reduce Stimulants:** Cut back on caffeine, sugar, and alcohol to support nervous system regulation.
- **Gut Health Support:** Add probiotic-rich foods like yogurt, kimchi, or fermented vegetables to aid digestion and emotional well-being.
- **Magnesium & B Vitamins:** Include leafy greens, nuts, and seeds to support stress reduction and nervous system health.
- **Mindful Eating:** Slow down, chew thoroughly, and pay attention to how food affects your mood.

After reviewing the checklist, reflect on where you might want to make additions to your diet to improve how it supports your healing:

_____
_____
_____
_____
_____
_____
_____
_____
_____

MINDFUL EATING EXERCISE

Mindful eating means being fully present with your food, savoring the flavors, and listening to your body's cues. It can help reduce emotional eating, improve digestion, and strengthen your connection to nourishment. This activity is a great way to reinforce healthy eating habits during your recovery. Just follow these steps:

1. **Step 1: Choose a Meal.** Pick one meal today to eat mindfully. It could be breakfast, lunch, dinner, or even a small snack.
2. **Step 2: Eliminate Distractions.** Put away your phone, TV, or any other distractions. Sit in a comfortable space and take a few deep breaths before starting.
3. **Step 3: Engage Your Senses.** As you eat, pay close attention to the following:
    a. Sight: What colors and textures do you notice on your plate?
    b. Smell: What aromas stand out? Take a moment to inhale deeply before taking a bite.
    c. Taste: Let each bite linger on your tongue. Can you pick up on different flavors?
    d. Texture: Is the food smooth, crunchy, or soft? How does it feel as you chew?
    e. Sound: If applicable, listen to the sounds of your food as you eat.
4. **Step 4: Listen to Your Body.**
    a. How hungry were you before you started eating? (Scale of 1–10)

    _____
    _____
    _____

    b. How do you feel as you eat? Are you satisfied, still hungry, or full?

    _____
    _____
    _____

    c. How does your mood shift throughout the meal?

    _____
    _____
    _____

5. **Step 5: Reflect on the Experience.** After you finish eating, take a moment to reflect:
    a. Did eating mindfully change how much you ate?

_____
_____
_____

b. Did you enjoy your food more?

_____
_____
_____

c. Did you notice any emotional connections to eating?

_____
_____
_____

Try this practice for different meals throughout the week and observe any changes in your relationship with food.

Sleep

Moving on to sleep, quality rest is another aspect of emotional well-being. Sleep is necessary for cognitive functions and emotional resilience. When we're sleep-deprived, our emotions can swing unpredictably, making us more prone to stress and less capable of handling life's ups and downs. Establishing a bedtime routine can significantly enhance both the quality and duration of your sleep. Simple habits like setting a consistent sleep schedule, creating a calming nighttime environment, and avoiding screens before bed can help prepare your body for rest.

To improve the quality of your sleep, it's helpful to engage in something called sleep hygiene, which refers to healthy habits surrounding sleep. Review this checklist to see some examples of good sleep hygiene, and then reflect in the space below about one area you'd like to improve:

- **Consistent Sleep Schedule:** Go to bed and wake up at the same time every day, even on weekends.
- **Screen-Free Wind-Down:** Avoid screens (phones, tablets, TVs) at least 30–60 minutes before bed.
- **Relaxing Pre-Sleep Routine:** Engage in calming activities like reading, meditation, or gentle stretching.

- **Comfortable Sleep Environment:** Keep your bedroom cool, dark, and quiet. Consider blackout curtains, white noise, or aromatherapy.
- **Limit Stimulants & Heavy Meals:** Avoid caffeine, alcohol, and large meals close to bedtime.
- **Get Natural Light During the Day:** Exposure to daylight helps regulate your sleep-wake cycle.
- **Use Your Bed for Sleep Only:** Avoid working or watching TV in bed to strengthen the brain's association between bed and sleep.
- **Journal or Brain Dump:** Write down any worries or to-do lists before bed to clear your mind.
- **Monitor Your Sleep Quality:** Track how rested you feel in the morning and adjust your habits as needed.

BEDTIME AFFIRMATION RITUAL

Incorporating affirmations into your bedtime routine can create a sense of calm, reduce nighttime anxiety, and promote restful sleep. You can achieve this by following the steps below:

1. **Step 1: Choose Your Affirmations.** Pick or create affirmations that resonate with you. Some examples include:
    a. "I am safe. My body is resting and healing."
    b. "I release today's worries and welcome peace."
    c. "I am grateful for this day and look forward to tomorrow."
    d. "I am worthy of rest, relaxation, and self-care."
    e. "I trust my body to restore itself while I sleep."
2. **Step 2: Create a Relaxing Atmosphere.**
    a. Dim the lights or light a candle.
    b. Play soft music or white noise if you find it soothing.
    c. Take deep breaths or do gentle stretches before lying down.

3. **Step 3: Repeat Your Affirmation.** Say your affirmation out loud or in your mind at least 3–5 times. Visualize yourself in a peaceful, restful state as you say it. If intrusive thoughts arise, gently bring your focus back to the affirmation.
4. **Step 4: Track Your Sleep Quality.** Use the space below to jot down how you feel before and after practicing this routine for a few nights:

   _____
   _____
   _____
   _____
   _____
   _____
   _____

5. **Step 5: Reflect on Your Experience.** After a week, consider:

   a. Did this practice help you fall asleep faster?

   _____
   _____
   _____
   _____

   b. Did you notice any difference in the quality of your sleep?

   _____
   _____
   _____
   _____

   c. Did repeating affirmations shift your mindset before bed?

   _____
   _____
   _____
   _____

This ritual can be adapted over time—experiment with different affirmations to see which feels most effective.

While it might seem challenging, prioritizing sleep and sticking to a regular sleep routine can make a noticeable difference in your daily life. Quality sleep helps the brain process emotions and memories, boosts problem-solving skills, and fortifies the immune system.

Integrating Physical Exercise

Engaging in regular physical activity has benefits for emotional resilience and mental health as well. Physical activity releases endorphins, which are natural mood lifters that help promote feelings of happiness. They have been known to alleviate symptoms of depression and anxiety, making exercise a valuable tool for emotional well-being.

Choosing activities you enjoy is essential for sustaining motivation and commitment. When you find joy in what you do, whether it's dancing, walking, or practicing yoga, it becomes easier to incorporate these activities into your everyday life. To help you pick an exercise or two that you find genuinely enjoyable, work through this activity:

1. **Reflect on Past Experiences:** What types of movement have you enjoyed in the past? Did you have a favorite physical activity as a child?

   _____
   _____
   _____

2. **Explore Your Preferences:** Do you prefer solo activities or group settings? Do you enjoy high-energy workouts (e.g., kickboxing) or calming movements (e.g., yoga)? Do you like being indoors or outdoors?

   _____
   _____
   _____

3. **Try Something New:** Choose one new activity you've never tried before but find interesting. Plan a time this week to give it a try.

   _____
   _____
   _____

4. **Set an Intentional Goal:** What's one small way you can add joyful movement to your daily routine? (e.g., Take a 10-minute walk after lunch or stretch before bed.)

Finding enjoyable activities encourages consistency rather than seeing exercise as a chore. This approach creates a more manageable routine where you look forward to moving your body. It is important to set specific times for exercise within your schedule, which aids in the development of consistent habits. This activity can help you create a strong exercise routine that fits seamlessly into your schedule:

1. **Assess Your Current Schedule:** When do you naturally have energy during the day? Are there specific time slots where you can fit in movement without stress?

   ----

2. **Choose Your Activities:** Pick 2-3 enjoyable activities (e.g., yoga, dancing, walking, strength training). Varying activities can keep your routine engaging.

   ----

3. **Set Realistic Goals:** How many days a week can you commit to movement? How long will each session be?

   ----

4. **Schedule It Like an Appointment:** Write down your chosen days and times for exercise. Treat this as a commitment to yourself, just like any other important task.

   ----

5. **Track and Adjust:** After one week, reflect: What worked? What didn't? Adjust the routine to make it more enjoyable and sustainable.

Regular Mental Health Check-ins

In exploring effective daily routines for emotional health, self-reflection and mindfulness practices are necessary. These practices empower us by allowing us to monitor our emotional states actively.

Routine Check-Ins

Routine check-ins that make it easier to pinpoint emotional fluctuations and identify triggers are a great choice to begin with. These check-ins offer awareness that creates the space necessary for adaptive coping strategies; for example, recognizing when certain situations or interactions trigger anxiety can prompt preemptive measures like deep breathing or seeking supportive conversations. It doesn't need to be complicated; you can use two minutes throughout the day for these check-ins and track them in the table below to help you connect patterns.

TIME/DATE	EMOTION	TRIGGER

Mindfulness Exercises

Mindfulness exercises, which include techniques such as breathing exercises and meditation, can ground you in the present moment. In turn, you can tune into your emotions without judgment and better regulate these emotions. Breathing exercises, for example, can be incredibly powerful in this context. Taking slow, deliberate breaths helps calm the nervous system, reduces stress, and enhances overall emotional regulation. One of my favorite mindful breathing exercises that I want to share with you is as follows:

1. Sit or lie down in a relaxed position. Close your eyes or soften your gaze.
2. Breathe in slowly through your nose, focusing on expanding your belly first, then your ribs, and finally your chest. Imagine your torso gently filling with air, like a balloon inflating.
3. Hold the breath for just a moment, allowing your body to absorb the sensation of fullness.
4. Release the air in reverse order—chest, ribs, belly—exhaling through your mouth. Imagine tension leaving your body with the breath.
5. With each cycle, notice any shifts in your physical or emotional state.
6. If your mind wanders, gently bring your focus back to your breath.

Emotional Health Jar

The Emotional Health Jar is a great self-care tool designed to support emotional well-being. Incorporating small, mindful habits into your daily routine means you can gain emotional resilience, reduce stress, and develop a sense of balance. For this activity, you'll need:

- A jar, box, or small container
- Small slips of paper or index cards
- A pen or marker
- (Optional) Decorative items to personalize your jar (stickers, paint, ribbon)

Then, follow these steps:

1. **Step 1: Prepare Your Jar.** Choose a jar or container that you can easily access each day. If you'd like, decorate it to make it more inviting and visually appealing. You can label it "Emotional Health Jar" or something more personal, like "Daily Care," "Mindful Moments," or "Self-Love Jar."
2. **Step 2: Brainstorm Emotional Well-Being Habits.** On small slips of paper, write down simple daily habits that support emotional health. These should be easy, actionable steps that help you feel grounded, relaxed, or uplifted. Here are some examples:
   a. Drink a calming tea before bed.
   b. Step outside for fresh air and take three deep breaths.
   c. Listen to a song that makes you feel happy or nostalgic.
   d. Write down three things you are grateful for.
   e. Spend five minutes stretching or doing light movement.
   f. Read a poem or inspiring quote.
   g. Light a candle and take a moment to reflect.
   h. Write a kind note to yourself.
   i. Do a 2-minute breathing exercise.
   j. Smile at yourself in the mirror and say an affirmation.

Aim to create at least 10–20 slips to begin with, and feel free to add more over time.

1. **Step 3: Fill Your Jar.** Fold each slip of paper and place it in your jar. If you like, you can categorize them by theme (e.g., relaxation, movement, mindfulness) using different colors of paper or writing.
2. **Step 4: Start Your Daily Habit.** Each morning (or whenever suits you best), draw one slip of paper from the jar. That will be your emotional well-being focus for the day. Try to complete the activity at some point before the day ends. If the habit doesn't fit into your day, you can modify it slightly or pick another one. The goal is to nurture yourself, not add pressure.

3. **Step 5: Reflect on Your Experience.** At the end of the day, take a moment to reflect:
    a. How did the activity impact your emotions?
    b. Did it help you feel more balanced, relaxed, or positive?
    c. Would you like to add new habits to the jar based on what you learned?
    d. You can also keep a journal alongside your jar to track your experiences over time.
4. **Step 6: Refresh and Customize.** As you grow in your emotional well-being journey, update your jar by:
    a. Adding new activities that you discover and enjoy
    b. Removing ones that no longer resonate with you
    c. Customizing based on seasons, moods, or specific needs (e.g., adding more cozy habits in winter)

The Emotional Health Jar is a flexible, low-pressure way to incorporate self-care into your routine. By making small, intentional choices each day, you can create lasting positive shifts in your emotional well-being.

Morning And Evening Routine Checklist

Putting all of the concepts in this chapter into practice might look overwhelming at first—we talked about a lot, after all! But don't worry; this process doesn't have to be challenging, and it can be as easy as creating a simple morning and evening routine checklist that supports your needs. Take a look at the sample checklists below, and then use the space below to modify or create a checklist of your own based on what we've discussed in this chapter.

MORNING ROUTINE CHECKLIST	EVENING ROUTINE CHECKLIST
• Hydrate: Drink a glass of water to wake up your body and mind. • Nourish: Eat a protein-rich breakfast to stabilize	• Screen-Free Time: Reduce exposure to screens at least 30–60 minutes before bed. • Light Dinner: Avoid heavy meals close to bedtime to aid digestion and improve sleep.

- blood sugar and support brain function.
- **Move Your Body:** Stretch, do yoga, or take a short walk to energize yourself.
- **Get Sunlight:** Step outside for a few minutes to help regulate your circadian rhythm.
- **Practice Mindfulness:** Do a short meditation, deep breathing, or grounding exercise.
- **Emotional Check-In:** Take a moment to assess your mood and set an intention for the day.

- **Relaxation Ritual:** Read, take a warm bath, journal, or do deep breathing exercises.
- **Sleep Environment:** Ensure your bedroom is cool, dark, and quiet.
- **Gratitude Reflection:** Write down one thing you are grateful for from the day.
- **Consistent Bedtime:** Go to bed at the same time every night to improve sleep quality.

Moving Forward

Wrapping up this chapter, we've talked about how important it is to set up daily routines that boost mental health. Nutrition and sleep play a big part in keeping our minds and emotions balanced. Eating brain-friendly foods and getting enough rest can help ward off mood swings and make life's challenges feel more manageable. And let's not forget about exercise—moving your body releases those happy chemicals that brighten your day. Embracing these practices may take effort, but they can lead to significant improvements in how we handle life's ups and downs.

Chapter Three

MINDFULNESS AND NEUROPLASTICITY— CHANGING THE NARRATIVE

Mindfulness and neuroplasticity are concepts that pave the way for healing and growth. Focusing on these approaches means that you can tap into your brain's natural ability to adapt and change. This chapter delves into how these practices can be especially beneficial for those who have experienced trauma by offering tools for recovery and subtly guiding you through a journey of self-discovery and resilience.

Understanding Neuroplasticity

Neuroplasticity, often referred to as brain plasticity, is a remarkable attribute of the human brain. It refers to your brain's ability to rewire itself by forming new connections. What makes it so important? This capability is the foundation that enables us to heal, grow, and change our mental processes. Working with different strategies can help you engage your brain in a way that uses neuroplasticity to create healthy thinking patterns and make space for growth.

Mindfulness Meditation

Incorporating small, mindful practices into your daily routine is a practical way to facilitate these neuroplasticity changes. Regular practice of mindfulness helps create an environment within the brain that supports healing and adaptation by freeing you up from rumination, unhealthy thinking patterns, or anxiety. These small steps, when made consistently, accumulate over time, gradually strengthening mental resilience.

A simple way to achieve this is through mindfulness meditation. You can find numerous guided meditations that focus on mindfulness online, but this meditation is one of my favorites and I recommend trying it for yourself:

1. Sit comfortably with your back straight but relaxed. Rest your hands on your lap or knees.
2. Close your eyes or soften your gaze. Take a slow, deep breath in through your nose, then exhale gently through your mouth.
3. Notice the feeling of the air entering and leaving your body. Observe any sounds in your environment without judgment. Feel the texture of your clothing, the weight of your body on the chair, or the sensation of your feet touching the ground.
4. If thoughts arise, simply notice them without attachment and gently bring your focus back to your breath and sensations.

After completing this meditation, take a moment to notice any shifts in your mood, tension levels, or mental clarity. How do you feel compared to before?

_____
_____
_____
_____
_____

ADDITIONAL MINDFULNESS EXERCISES FOR NEUROPLASTICITY

If meditation isn't your preferred method for mindfulness, other activities can be beneficial as well! For example, you can work with this gratitude rewiring exercise that helps create new neural connections:

1. Take a few deep breaths and settle into a comfortable position.
2. Think of three things you are grateful for today. They can be big or small—anything that brought you joy, comfort, or peace.
3. As you reflect on each one, visualize it clearly in your mind. Feel the emotions that arise—happiness, warmth, contentment.
4. To deepen the impact, write them down in a journal or say them aloud. Notice how your body and mind respond to this practice.

Repeating this exercise daily can help train your brain to focus on positive experiences, reducing stress and increasing resilience over time.

Another excellent mindfulness activity you can work with is a sensory grounding walk. This activity helps ground you in the present moment while engaging your senses, encouraging new neural connections through heightened awareness:

1. Step outside or find a peaceful indoor space where you can move around. Walk slowly and deliberately. As you move, focus on one sense at a time:
    a. **Sight:** Notice the colors, shapes, and movements around you.
    b. **Sound:** Listen to distant and nearby sounds without labeling them.
    c. **Touch:** Feel the ground beneath your feet, the air on your skin.
    d. **Smell:** Breathe in deeply and identify any scents in the air.
2. If your mind wanders, gently redirect your focus to your surroundings.
3. After a few minutes, pause and take a deep breath. Reflect on how your body and mind feel after engaging in this sensory experience.

Visualization

Now, let's explore visualization techniques. Visualization isn't just daydreaming; it's an incredible practice used to help visualize positive neural changes. When you spend time imagining desired changes or outcomes, you stimulate the same brain areas that would be involved if you were actually experiencing those changes. For example, athletes often use visualization to enhance performance, picturing themselves succeeding before they perform. In the context of healing, visualizing oneself feeling safe, calm, and in control can empower individuals to create those same feelings in reality. In the space below, write down one visualization you'd like to try that would make you feel more secure—

such as being in a safe place or with people you trust. Then, engage with the visualization for 3–5 minutes and reflect on your experience.

_____
_____
_____
_____
_____
_____

To make the most of neuroplasticity, having practical guidelines can be incredibly beneficial. When it comes to integrating mindfulness practices into everyday life, start small. Devote just a few minutes each day to mindfulness meditation or focused breathing exercises. Consistency is key, so build it into your routine like brushing your teeth or having a morning coffee.

Shifting Mental Pathways

Creating new mental pathways can greatly aid trauma recovery. The first step in this process is recognizing the unhelpful mental pathways that have been formed as a result of trauma. These pathways, ingrained by repeated thoughts and behaviors over time, often manifest in negative self-talk or harmful habits. Acknowledging their presence highlights the need for change and motivates individuals to seek healthier alternatives. This awareness sets the stage for forming new neural paths.

Shifting these pathways can sound complicated, but it doesn't have to be—it just takes consistency. You can begin the process with this activity:

1. **Identify a Common Negative Thought:** Write down one recurring negative thought you have about yourself or your abilities.

    _____
    _____
    _____

2. **Recognize the Trigger:** Reflect on when this thought usually arises.

_____
_____
_____

3. **Challenge the Thought:** Ask yourself—is this absolutely true? What evidence do I have against this belief?

   _____
   _____
   _____

4. **Replace It With a Healthier Thought:** Create a new, more balanced statement to practice.

   _____
   _____
   _____

5. **Reinforce Through Repetition:** Each time the negative thought appears, consciously replace it with your new statement. Write your new thought on a sticky note or repeat it aloud daily.

Developing New Pathways

Techniques for developing these new, healthier pathways heavily rely on consistent mindfulness practices. Mindfulness helps in observing thoughts without judgment, allowing individuals to detach from old patterns and cultivate a fresh perspective. For example, when feelings of anxiety arise, mindfulness encourages us to acknowledge the emotion, explore its roots, and then gently guide our thoughts toward calming affirmations.

New Habits

The principle "neurons that fire together wire together" is central to forming new habits through repetition. This concept, introduced by psychologist Donald Hebb, suggests that the brain strengthens connections between neurons that frequently activate simultaneously (Dr, 2010). In practical terms, this means that by repeatedly engaging in positive activities—like gratitude journaling or daily meditative practices—we encourage our brains to fortify these beneficial pathways. Over time, these actions become easier and more automatic, slowly replacing the less helpful habits hardwired by past traumas.

There's no better time than the present to get started with a new habit, especially when that habit helps you grow. Based on what you've learned so far about mindfulness and its potential for healing, write down one habit you want to pick up and how you think it'll benefit you. Then, schedule time to practice it daily, and reflect on how the habit impacts you over time. Don't be afraid to readjust your goal if needed!

Celebrating Progress

Celebrating progress is another component in reinforcing effort and maintaining motivation. Acknowledging even minor achievements provides emotional fuel to continue the journey. Whether it's managing stress better one day or simply completing a week of mindfulness practice, celebrating these victories helps solidify new pathways by associating them with a sense of accomplishment and joy. Consider rewarding yourself with simple pleasures, such as a favorite hobby or a quiet moment of reflection, to reinforce the positive behavior.

Engaging Your Inner Child For New Pathways

Your inner child isn't an actual person, but it does represent the emotions and experiences you had as a child and carry with you to this day. Part of creating new pathways means addressing what created the original pathways, and inner child work is beneficial for this. For example, if you faced neglect during childhood, you can "re-parent" your inner child to heal the wounds left by neglect. These activities are geared toward helping you engage with your inner child for enhanced healing.

REPARENTING LETTER TO YOUR INNER CHILD

One of the most powerful ways to heal from complex trauma is through reparenting—offering your younger self the love, validation, and reassurance they may not have received. This exercise helps rewire emotional pathways by replacing self-criticism and fear with self-compassion and security.

1. Find a quiet, comfortable space.
2. Close your eyes and visualize your younger self at an age when they needed comfort the most. Imagine them sitting across from you.
3. Write a compassionate letter from your present self to your inner child. Include affirmations like:
    a. "You are loved."
    b. "You are safe with me."
    c. "What happened to you was not your fault."
    d. "I will take care of you now."
4. If emotions arise, allow them without judgment.
5. Read the letter aloud and reflect on any shifts in emotion or self-perception.

You can use this space to write your letter:

_____
_____
_____
_____
_____
_____
_____
_____
_____
_____
_____
_____
_____
_____

Over time, repeating this practice helps your brain replace negative internalized beliefs with self-compassion, strengthening healthier emotional pathways.

INNER CHILD VISUALIZATION: A SAFE HAVEN

Our brains naturally respond to imagery, and by creating a mental space of safety, we can help rewire trauma responses and develop a greater sense of inner peace. This visualization exercise allows you to connect with your inner child in a way that elevates security, self-acceptance, and emotional regulation.

1. Find a quiet space and sit or lie down comfortably.
2. Close your eyes and take a few deep breaths, grounding yourself in the present moment.
3. Imagine a safe and peaceful place—this could be a cozy childhood bedroom, a forest, or a warm beach.
4. Now, picture your younger self in this space. See them exploring, playing, or simply resting.
5. Approach them gently and offer a comforting gesture—a hug, holding their hand, or simply sitting with them.
6. Whisper kind words to them, reassuring them that they are safe and cared for.
7. When ready, take a deep breath and slowly return to the present moment.

This practice helps rewire the brain's responses to past distress by reinforcing a sense of security and self-soothing.

RECONNECTING THROUGH CREATIVITY

Engaging in childhood-like play is more than just fun—it activates neural pathways associated with joy, curiosity, and spontaneity, helping to counteract the rigid thought patterns formed by trauma. This activity encourages emotional flexibility and reinforces the idea that safety and pleasure can coexist.

1. Set aside 20–30 minutes to do something purely playful:
    a. Finger painting or coloring with crayons
    b. Building with Legos or blocks
    c. Blowing bubbles outside
    d. Dancing freely to nostalgic music

      e. Playing a simple game like hopscotch or skipping stones
2. While engaging, pay attention to your emotions and body sensations. If resistance or guilt arises, gently remind yourself that play is a form of healing.
3. Afterward, journal about how you felt during and after the activity.

Moving Forward

Remember that harnessing mindfulness and neuroplasticity can be incredibly helpful in the path of trauma healing. We've explored how our brains can reshape themselves and open doors to new ways of thinking and feeling. Incorporating mindful practices like meditation and visualization into daily life allows you to gently steer your mind toward healthier pathways.

It's important to approach this concept with patience and compassion for yourself. Small, consistent efforts count. While it's not always easy, taking time for mindfulness and focusing on positive imagery can gradually build mental strength and clarity. Embrace these moments as opportunities for growth, knowing that each mindful breath and every effort to develop new neural pathways brings you closer to thriving beyond survival.

Chapter Four

CREATING YOUR PERSONAL RESILIENCE ACTION PLAN

Creating your Personal Resilience Action Plan means taking charge of your mental well-being and creating a path tailored to your unique needs and experiences. Navigating this process means understanding your values deeply, setting goals that resonate with you, and utilizing every resource available to enhance your mental health toolkit. This chapter invites you to explore various strategies that can elevate your resilience.

Setting Personal Goals

Establishing clear personal goals is important for providing direction and motivation in developing resilience. An effective strategy for setting these goals is through the SMART criteria—an acronym that stands for specific, measurable, achievable, relevant, and time-bound objectives. But what does this all mean? Let's break it down!

- S — **Specific.** A goal must be specific. For example, instead of expressing a vague desire to improve mental well-being, a more specific goal might be attending therapy sessions weekly for the next three months.
- M — **Measurable.** The measurable criterion ensures that your progress can be tracked.
- A — **Achievable.** The achievable aspect focuses on setting realistic goals that, while challenging, remain within your capabilities.

- **R — Relevant.** Next, ensuring relevance means aligning your goals with personal values and long-term aspirations. F
- **T — Time-bound.** Finally, the goal should be time-bound, stipulating a clear timeframe to create healthy urgency and maintain focus.

With this in mind, try setting a SMART goal below:

1. What is your main goal? Write it down below.

   _____
   _____
   _____

2. Is this goal specific? How?

   _____
   _____
   _____
   _____

3. Is this goal measurable? How?

   _____
   _____
   _____

4. Is this goal achievable? How?

   _____
   _____
   _____

5. Is this goal relevant? How?

   _____
   _____
   _____

6. Is this goal time-bound? How?

   _____
   _____
   _____
   _____

7. If needed, modify your goal to fit the SMART framework.

Differentiating between short- and long-term goals enables you to enjoy small victories while keeping sight of bigger dreams. Undoubtedly, you have a few things you already want to achieve. In the table below, fill out some of your long- and short-term goals. Don't feel pressured to fill out the entire table if you want to focus on one or two goals for now.

LONG- OR SHORT-TERM?	GOAL	MEETS SMART FRAMEWORK?	ACTION STEPS	NOTES/ REFLECTIONS

Long-Term Vision Planning

Having a clear long-term vision is ideal because it gives you something to use to remind yourself of why you're working so hard. Developing this vision involves using creative tools, imagination exercises, and strategic planning to map out your personal path.

Vision Board

Creating a vision board is an excellent starting point. Vision boards can help you express long-term aspirations and life goals creatively. Selecting images, words, and symbols that resonate with your desires is a way to create a physical reminder of what you're striving toward.

To construct a vision board, begin by collecting materials that speak to your dreams. You can include pictures of places you'd like to visit, quotes that inspire you, or representations of career achievements you aspire to reach. The act of curating these elements helps clarify your intentions and reinforces positive thinking. From there, assemble your board—it can be done on poster board, digitally, or even assorted as a collection of items in a shoebox if you prefer. After creating your vision board, reflect on why you picked each element, what it means to you, and how it inspires you:

Personal Mission Statement

A personal mission statement further solidifies this vision. This requires you to articulate your core values and the purpose driving your actions. In crafting this statement, consider questions such as what matters most to you and how you want to impact the world around you. It should include why you want to heal and what you want to achieve, as well as how you'll strive for it. Create your mission statement in the space below:

_____
_____
_____
_____
_____

Imagining Your Future Self

Imagining your future self is another powerful exercise in building your long-term vision. Give it a try:

1. Sit comfortably in a calm environment where you won't be disturbed.
2. Inhale slowly through your nose, hold for a moment, and exhale gently. Repeat until you feel centered.
3. Imagine yourself five, ten, or twenty years from now. Picture your surroundings—where are you? Consider what you are doing and who is with you. Notice how you feel in this future moment.
4. Write down or draw what you envisioned. Include specific details about your future self's mindset, habits, and accomplishments.

   _____
   _____
   _____
   _____

5. Identify one action you can take today to move toward this vision.

   _____
   _____
   _____

This imaginative process provides clarity on what you truly desire and can show you what pathways to take to get there. For example, if you visualize yourself living in a peaceful countryside home pursuing a different career, it might indicate a need for lifestyle changes now. Recognizing these aspirations helps you set intentional milestones today. It's a practice in foresight, helping you align current actions with future outcomes ("How to Create a Life Plan (a Life Planning Template)", 2021).

Utilizing Support Resources

When developing a personal resilience action plan, identifying and utilizing support resources can be game-changing for strengthening resilience and recovery efforts. This involves recognizing both professional therapeutic support as well as community-driven and online resources that can provide guidance and help you achieve a growth-oriented mindset.

Therapy

For many women who have experienced trauma, engaging in consistent therapy sessions can offer guidance and coping strategies tailored to our needs. Be it talk therapy, dialectical behavioral therapy, or cognitive processing therapy, professional help provides structured techniques to navigate complex emotions and past experiences effectively (*MHI - Mental Health Incorporation*, 2024).

Community-Driven Programs And Resources

An important part of resilience-building is reaching out to local community resources. Community-driven programs can provide a sense of connection and shared experience that can be immensely beneficial during the recovery process. These programs include peer support groups, workshops, and events that bring people together in a safe space to share stories and strategies. Such environments promote healing by normalizing experiences and reducing feelings of isolation.

It can be a bit tricky to find community-driven programs in some areas, but often, a little research is all you need to find such programs. Try each of the following search terms, and then take some notes about what you find in the space below. Note down any options you're especially interested in, when they meet, and how to attend before committing to attending one program if you feel comfortable doing so. Some search terms you can try include:

- Trauma recovery group near me
- Trauma support group near me
- C-PTSD groups near me

- Self-improvement group near me
- Self-improvement workshops near me

You can use the lines below to jot down your research:

_____
_____
_____
_____
_____
_____
_____
_____
_____
_____

Digital Options

With the rise of technology, online support platforms have become increasingly popular as they provide convenient access to resources and peer communities. Online forums, social media groups, and virtual therapy sessions allow us to connect with others who share similar challenges, regardless of their geographical location—all from the comfort of your home and with any level of anonymity you prefer. Sites like Facebook, Reddit, and similar have dedicated communities for healing and recovery, including when it comes to C-PTSD. Take a look at the groups available online and jot down which ones seem promising based on their community, rules, and atmosphere.

_____
_____
_____
_____
_____
_____
_____
_____
_____

Literature And Workshops

Self-help literature and workshops are also valuable in enhancing understanding and supporting a growth-oriented mindset. Books on resilience and trauma recovery can equip you with knowledge about psychological processes and introduce you to new coping mechanisms. Workshops, whether live or online, provide opportunities to learn through interactive activities and expert discussions. For example, attending a mindfulness workshop might give someone practical exercises they can incorporate into their daily routine to reduce stress and increase emotional resilience.

Action Plan Worksheet

If you're still feeling stuck on how to create your resilience action plan, this fill-in-the-blank worksheet can make the process easier:

My Personal Goal: One specific goal I want to achieve for my mental well-being is:

I want to _____ by _____ (timeframe).

SMART Goal Breakdown:

- My goal is specific because:

  _____.

- My goal is measurable because:

  _____.

- My goal is achievable because:

  _____.

- My goal is relevant to my well-being because:

  _____.

- My goal is time-bound because:

  _____.

Long-Term Vision:

One major long-term goal I have for my life is:

_____.

One action I can take today to move toward this goal is:

_____.

Support Resources:

One local resource or community program I found that could support me is:

_____.

One online group, forum, or digital resource I plan to explore is:

_____.

Personal Mission Statement:

The values most important to me are:

_____.

My mission in healing and personal growth is:

_____.

Imagining My Future Self:

In 5–10 years, I see myself:

_____.

One step I can take now to move toward this vision is:

_____.

Commitment to Growth:

One habit or daily practice I will start to build resilience is:

_____.

> One thing I will remind myself when facing challenges is:
>
> _____.

Moving Forward

In this chapter, we've discussed practical ways to set and achieve personal goals that boost resilience while maintaining mental health. By using the SMART criteria, you can create goals that are specific, measurable, achievable, relevant, and time-bound. This approach provides a clear direction and gives you motivation as you track your progress. We've also looked at breaking down goals into short-term and long-term targets.

Beyond goal-setting, it's helpful to think about how to harness support resources effectively. Utilizing professional therapy, community networks, and online platforms can provide the support you need and deserve to navigate challenges. These tools enable you to build connections, gain new understandings, and practice exercises that enhance emotional strength. Remember, building resilience isn't just about reaching goals—it's about creating a meaningful journey that aligns with your deepest values and aspirations.

Chapter Five

ADDITIONAL METHODS FOR CONTINUED GROWTH

After exploring resilience, daily habits for healthy healing, and so much more, there are a few more helpful methods we have to touch on to round out your journey. Specifically, in this chapter, we're going to cover how you can share your story with others to empower yourself and them in recovery, what you can do to support others on a similar path to yours when you feel ready to do so, how you can ask for help as you recover, and how to monitor your progress in truly impactful ways—all through practical activities you can work through and repeat as often as needed.

Supporting Others On Their Journey

Telling your personal story can be a powerful tool for both your own healing and for inspiring others. When we share our experiences, we validate our struggles, enhance connection, and give others hope. This activity will help you craft your story in a way that is empowering and uplifting, which can help you by allowing for reflection, release, and support, and help others by seeing that growth and recovery is possible through your story of resilience.

Activity: Crafting Your Healing Narrative

1. Reflect on Your Journey: Write about your experiences with C-PTSD. What challenges have you faced? What milestones have you achieved?

_____
_____
_____
_____

2. **Identify Key Lessons:** What insights have you gained? What would you tell someone at the beginning of their healing journey?

   _____
   _____
   _____

3. **Frame It With Strength:** Focus on your resilience. Instead of just detailing struggles, highlight moments of growth and transformation.

   _____
   _____
   _____

4. **Decide What to Share:** Determine which parts of your story you feel comfortable sharing with others. Boundaries are important.

   _____
   _____
   _____

5. **Practice Sharing:** Write or record your story and rehearse sharing it in a way that feels authentic but safe for you.

   _____
   _____
   _____
   _____
   _____

Supporting Others: An Idea Checklist

Supporting others is absolutely worthwhile, but it can be hard to know where to start, especially when it comes to something as significant as healing from C-PTSD. My favorite thing to consider is what I needed most on my journey; chances are, others have similar needs. However, you can also use this checklist to pick options:

- **Active Listening:** Offer a nonjudgmental space for them to share their thoughts and feelings.
- **Validation:** Acknowledge their experiences without minimizing or offering unsolicited advice.
- **Encouragement:** Remind them of their strength and progress, even when they don't see it.
- **Respecting Boundaries:** Allow them to set their own pace and respect their personal limits.
- **Providing Resources:** Share books, articles, or support groups that might be helpful.
- **Helping With Practical Needs:** Offer assistance with daily tasks if they are struggling.
- **Being a Consistent Presence:** Show up and check in regularly, even in small ways.
- **Offering Distractions:** Engage in enjoyable activities together to bring lightness into their life.
- **Encouraging Professional Help:** If they are open to it, suggest therapy or other professional support.
- **Practicing Patience:** Understand that healing is nonlinear and requires time.

If you have someone in your life who you're working to support, pick one of the above methods and commit to helping in that way. Remember to ask if you can help before forcing help on others, though—some people prefer to be more independent. With that said, try to help someone out on their journey and reflect on the experience below.

_____
_____
_____
_____
_____
_____
_____

_____
_____

Supporting Others While Maintaining Your Well-Being

Helping others heal can be deeply fulfilling, but it's important to do so in a way that maintains your well-being. This activity will help you explore ways to offer support while protecting your energy.

Activity: Defining Your Role as a Supporter

1. **Assess Your Capacity:** How much emotional energy can you realistically offer others while maintaining your own well-being?
   _____
   _____
   _____

2. **Set Boundaries:** What topics or situations feel too triggering for you to engage with?
   _____
   _____
   _____

3. **Choose Your Support Style:** Do you prefer one-on-one conversations, online support groups, or advocacy work?
   _____
   _____
   _____

4. **Create an Action Plan:** List ways you can support others (e.g., sharing resources, listening, guiding someone to professional help).
   _____
   _____
   _____

5. **Check in With Yourself:** Regularly evaluate whether supporting others is uplifting or overwhelming for you.

Asking For Help When You Need It

Seeking support is a sign of strength. Supporting others is incredible, but you can't forget to take time to support yourself—which includes asking for help when you need it. Everyone needs help sometimes, and while the process of asking can be daunting, this activity will guide you through identifying and reaching out for help when needed.

Activity: Building Your Support Network

1. **List Your Trusted People:** Write down friends, family, or professionals who can support you.

2. **Identify What You Need:** Do you need emotional support, practical help, or guidance?

3. **Practice Reaching Out:** Draft a message or script asking for help in a way that feels natural to you.

4. **Address Fear of Asking:** Reflect on any discomfort around seeking help and challenge any limiting beliefs.

5. **Set a Goal:** Choose one person to reach out to this week for support.

   _____
   _____
   _____

Performing Regular Progress Checks

Tracking your healing journey helps you see growth and identify areas needing attention. This activity provides a structured way to assess your progress.

Activity: Monthly Healing Check-In

1. **Rate Your Well-Being:** On a scale of 1-10, how are you feeling emotionally, mentally, and physically?

   _____
   _____
   _____

2. **Identify Wins:** What positive changes have you noticed in yourself recently?

   _____
   _____
   _____

3. **Acknowledge Challenges:** What struggles have surfaced, and how have you handled them?

   _____
   _____
   _____

4. **Set Intentions:** What small steps can you take in the next month to continue healing?

   _____
   _____
   _____

5. **Reflect on Support:** Are you giving and receiving enough support? If not, what adjustments can you make?

Activity: Emotional Check-In Wheel

This activity helps track your emotional well-being over time, which makes it easier to recognize patterns and identify triggers. Visually mapping your emotions means that you can better understand your healing journey and notice when certain feelings are becoming more frequent. For this activity, you'll need a blank sheet of paper, colored pencils, markers, or a digital drawing app, and optionally, a ruler.

1. Draw the Wheel:
   a. On your paper, draw a large circle.
   b. Divide the circle into 30 sections (one for each day of the month). If that's too much, you can divide it into weeks instead.
   c. Each section represents a daily or weekly check-in.
2. Label Your Emotions:
   a. Create a key with different emotions you frequently experience (e.g., calm, anxious, hopeful, overwhelmed, angry, peaceful).
   b. Assign each emotion a color.
   c. If you are unsure which emotions to track, start with basic categories like:
      i. Positive emotions: Peaceful, joyful, hopeful, accomplished
      ii. Neutral emotions: Tired, indifferent, numb
      iii. Challenging emotions: Anxious, sad, angry, frustrated
3. Daily Check-In:
   a. At the end of each day, take a few minutes to reflect on how you felt overall.
   b. Color in the section for that day with the emotion that stood out most. If multiple emotions were strong, blend colors or add patterns.
4. Reflect After a Month:
   a. After 30 days (or at the end of the time period you chose), look at your wheel.
   b. Ask yourself:
      i. What emotions appear most often?

      ii. Are there any patterns related to your mood shifts?

      iii. Do certain situations, people, or activities influence specific emotions?

      iv. What days or weeks were the hardest? The most uplifting?

      v. How can you use this awareness to adjust your healing journey?

5. **Use the Data for Healing:**
   a. If you notice many negative emotions, think about introducing coping strategies (journaling, grounding techniques, therapy, or social support).
   b. If positive emotions are increasing, celebrate the progress and identify what's working for you.
   c. Keep repeating this activity monthly to track long-term healing.
6. **Reflection Prompt:** What did this exercise reveal about your emotional patterns? How can you use this awareness to support your healing process?

Guided Compassion Meditation

Healing from C-PTSD often involves self-criticism and struggles with self-worth. This guided meditation focuses on building compassion—both for yourself and for others who are on their own healing paths. It leads to a sense of connection, reduces shame, and nurtures inner kindness.

1. **Find a Comfortable Position:** Sit or lie down in a way that allows your body to fully relax. Close your eyes and take a few deep, slow breaths. Feel your body settling.
2. **Ground Yourself in the Present Moment:** Bring your attention to your breath. Inhale deeply for a count of four, hold for four, then exhale slowly for four. As you breathe, visualize tension leaving your body.
3. **Send Compassion to Yourself:** Place your hand over your heart. Imagine a warm, golden light filling your chest, radiating outward. As this light grows, repeat silently or aloud:
    a. "I am worthy of healing."
    b. "I am learning to be kind to myself."
    c. "I give myself the same compassion I would give a dear friend."
    d. Stay with this feeling for a minute or two. If self-critical thoughts arise, acknowledge them, then gently return to the warmth of compassion.
4. **Extend Compassion to Others:** Picture someone else who is also struggling with C-PTSD or emotional healing. Imagine sending the same golden light to them, offering kindness and understanding. Silently say:
    a. "May you find peace and strength."
    b. "You are not alone in your journey."
    c. "May you be surrounded by love and healing."
5. **Return to Yourself and Close the Meditation:** Slowly bring your attention back to your breath. Wiggle your fingers and toes, bringing awareness back to your body. Open your eyes and take a deep breath, feeling present and refreshed.
6. **Reflection Prompt:** How did this meditation feel? Did you find it easier to offer compassion to yourself or others? How can you bring more self-compassion into your daily healing journey?

_____
_____
_____
_____

Moving Forward

Engaging in these activities means that you can use your story, support others, and maintain a strong sense of stability for your own healing journey. These techniques make healing easier and also provide more fulfillment—healing doesn't have to happen alone, whether you're supporting others or asking them to support you.

Conclusion

Healing from complex PTSD is not a linear path, nor is it a destination—it is a continuous journey of growth, self-discovery, and resilience. Throughout this book, you have explored how to strengthen your emotional foundation through daily habits, mindfulness, neuroplasticity, and intentional self-care. You have also crafted a Personal Resilience Action Plan, a tool that will help guide you in maintaining the progress you've made and adapting to new challenges with confidence.

As you move forward, remember that resilience is not about never struggling—it is about how you respond to those struggles. Some days will feel lighter than others, and setbacks may happen, but each step you take toward emotional well-being is meaningful. Healing is not about perfection; it's about showing up for yourself, even in small ways, every day.

You are not defined by your past. You are capable, strong, and worthy of a future built on self-trust and empowerment. Carry the lessons you've learned here into your daily life, and know that no matter where you are in your journey, you have the power to keep moving forward.

References

Book 1

Barriga, P. A. (2022). *Embracing the Reality of Trauma and its Impact in Career Development*. Ncda.org. https://www.ncda.org/aws/NCDA/pt/sd/news_article/424713/_PARENT/CC_layout_details/crc32

Calhoun, C. D., Stone, K. J., Cobb, A. R., Patterson, M. W., Danielson, C. K., & Bendezú, J. J. (2022, October 5). *The Role of Social Support in Coping with Psychological Trauma: An Integrated Biopsychosocial Model for Posttraumatic Stress Recovery*. Psychiatric Quarterly. https://doi.org/10.1007/s11126-022-10003-w

CPTSD (Complex PTSD). (2023, April 5). Cleveland Clinic. https://my.clevelandclinic.org/health/diseases/24881-cptsd-complex-ptsd

Devastatingly pervasive: 1 in 3 Women Globally Experience Violence. (2021, March 9). World Health Organization. https://www.who.int/news/item/09-03-2021-devastatingly-pervasive-1-in-3-women-globally-experience-violence

DiGonis, E. (n.d.). *The Power of Journaling: Structured Approaches for Trauma Recovery | CPTSDfoundation.org*. https://cptsdfoundation.org/2023/08/02/the-power-of-journaling-structured-approaches-for-trauma-recovery/

Downey, C., & Crummy, A. (2021). *The impact of childhood trauma on children's well-being and adult behavior*. European Journal of Trauma & Dissociation. https://doi.org/10.1016/j.ejtd.2021.100237

elizablooms. (2023, July 15). *Why Healing Trauma Starts With Creating Safety (& How to Feel Safe Again)*. Eliza Blooms. https://elizablooms.com/2023/07/16/why-healing-trauma-starts-with-creating-safety-feeling-safe-after-trauma/

Ford, J. D., Grasso, D. J., Elhai, J. D., & Courtois, C. A. (2015). *Social, cultural, and Other Diversity Issues in the Traumatic Stress Field*. Posttraumatic Stress Disorder. https://doi.org/10.1016/B978-0-12-801288-8.00011-X

French, M. (2024, April 5). *C-PTSD vs. PTSD: How do they differ?* Medicalnewstoday.com; Medical News Today. https://www.medicalnewstoday.com/articles/cptsd-vs-ptsd

Lanius, R. A., Terpou, B. A., & McKinnon, M. C. (2020). *The sense of self in the aftermath of trauma: lessons from the default mode network in posttraumatic stress disorder*. European Journal of Psychotraumatology. https://doi.org/10.1080/20008198.2020.1807703

Lebow, H. (2021, June 10). *Do Your Early Experiences Affect Your Adult Relationships?* Psych Central. https://psychcentral.com/blog/how-childhood-trauma-affects-adult-relationships

Lee, M. (2023, July 31). *Breaking Down Barriers: Navigating the Cultural Impact on Child Abuse Cases*. NCACIA Protection. https://www.ncacia.org/post/breaking-down-barriers-navigating-the-cultural-impact-on-child-abuse-cases

Li, Y., & Liang, Y. (2023, October 31). *The effect of childhood trauma on complex posttraumatic stress disorder: the role of self-esteem*. European Journal of Psychotraumatology; Taylor & Francis. https://doi.org/10.1080/20008066.2023.2272478

Lopes, S. (2021, May 12). *Unhealed trauma may be killing your career. Why mental healing should be part of your career strategy - The Corporate Sister*. The Corporate Sister. https://www.thecorporatesister.com/blog/unhealed-trauma-may-be-killing-your-career-why-mental-healing-should-be-part-of-your-career-strategy/

Mark, K. P., Vowels, L. M., Mullis, L., & Hoskins, K. (2023, September 6). *Women's strategies for navigating a healthy sex life post-sexual trauma*. PLOS ONE; Public Library of Science. https://doi.org/10.1371/journal.pone.0291011

Mayo Clinic Staff. (2023). *Support groups: Make connections, get help*. Mayo Clinic. https://www.mayoclinic.org/healthy-lifestyle/stress-management/in-depth/support-groups/art-20044655

National Library of Medicine. (2001). *Culture Counts: The Influence of Culture and Society on Mental Health*. National Library of Medicine; Substance Abuse and Mental Health Services Administration (US). https://www.ncbi.nlm.nih.gov/books/NBK44249/

Nayara Ribeiro Slompo, Aline Martins Alves, Chociay, S., Guilherme Tosi Feitosa, Santos, Bruna Moretti Luchesi, & Martins, T. (2023, June 5). *Factors Associated with Symptoms of Posttraumatic Stress in Mothers During the COVID-19 Pandemic*. Maternal and Child Health Journal; Springer Science+Business Media. https://doi.org/10.1007/s10995-023-03723-3

Novotney, A. (2023, April 13). *Women who experience trauma are twice as likely as men to develop PTSD. Here's why*. Apa.org; American Psychological Association. https://www.apa.org/topics/women-girls/women-trauma

Sinko, L., Schaitkin, C., & Saint Arnault, D. (2021, January). *The Healing after Gender-Based Violence Scale (GBV-Heal): An Instrument to Measure Recovery Progress in Women-Identifying Survivors*. Global Qualitative Nursing Research. https://doi.org/10.1177/2333393621996679

Truitt, K. (2023, November 8). *Navigating Trauma: How to Build Your Emotional Safe Space*. Dr. Kate Truitt & Associates. https://drtruitt.com/navigating-trauma-how-to-build-your-emotional-safe-space/

Ven, M. C. J., Heuvel, M. I., Bhogal, A., Lewis, T., & Thomason, M. E. (2019, August). *Impact of maternal childhood trauma on child behavioral problems: The role of child frontal alpha asymmetry*. Developmental Psychobiology. https://doi.org/10.1002/dev.21900

Wal, J. V. (2024, August 9). The Healing Power of Journaling | GR Therapy Group. GR Therapy Group. https://grandrapidstherapygroup.com/journaling-addressing-trauma-through-writing/

What is complex PTSD? (2021, January). Mind. https://www.mind.org.uk/information-support/types-of-mental-health-problems/post-traumatic-stress-disorder-ptsd-and-complex-ptsd/complex-ptsd/

Zhang, X., & Yan, E. (2024, November 1). *The Impact of Maternal Childhood Trauma on Children's Problem Behaviors: The Mediating Role of Maternal Depression and the Moderating Role of Mindful Parenting*. Psychology Research and Behavior Management; Dove Medical Press. https://doi.org/10.2147/prbm.s485821

Book 2

Ackerman, C. (2017, March 20). *25 CBT Techniques and Worksheets for Cognitive Behavioral Therapy.* PositivePsychology.com. https://positivepsychology.com/cbt-cognitive-behavioral-therapy-techniques-worksheets/

Ankrom, S. (2024, February 16). *Need a Breather? Try These 9 Breathing Exercises to Relieve Anxiety.* Verywell Mind. https://www.verywellmind.com/abdominal-breathing-2584115

Center for Substance Abuse Treatment. (2014). *Understanding the impact of trauma.* National Library of Medicine; Substance Abuse and Mental Health Services Administration (US). https://www.ncbi.nlm.nih.gov/books/NBK207191/

Copley, L. (2023, November 30). 30 Best Journaling Prompts for Improving Mental Health. PositivePsychology.com. https://positivepsychology.com/journaling-prompts/

DiGonis, E. (n.d.). *The Power of Journaling: Structured Approaches for Trauma Recovery | CPTSDfoundation.org.* https://cptsdfoundation.org/2023/08/02/the-power-of-journaling-structured-approaches-for-trauma-recovery/

Grounding Techniques for Effective Anxiety and Stress Relief - Resilience Lab. (n.d.). Www.resiliencelab.us. https://www.resiliencelab.us/thought-lab/grounding-techniques

Karimova, H. (2018, March 5). *7 Best Mood Tracker Ideas For Your Bullet Journal Mood Charts (+PDFs).* PositivePsychology.com. https://positivepsychology.com/mood-charts-track-your-mood/

Lee, M. (2023, August 2). *Adverse Childhood Experiences: Navigating the Impact on Adult Life.* NCACIA Protection. https://www.ncacia.org/post/adverse-childhood-experiences-navigating-the-impact-on-adult-life

Lupcho, T. (2023, October 13). *Domestic Violence Therapy Guide | Thriveworks.* Https://Thriveworks.com/. https://thriveworks.com/therapy/domestic-violence-therapy/

Mayo Clinic Staff. (2022). *Relaxation techniques: Try these steps to reduce stress.* Mayo Clinic. https://www.mayoclinic.org/healthy-lifestyle/stress-management/in-depth/relaxation-technique/art-20045368

McKenna, K. (n.d.). *Distraction Techniques for Anxiety*. Kelly McKenna - SIT with KELLY. https://www.sitwithkelly.com/blog/distraction-techniques

Monfared, J. (2023). *Childhood Trauma and its effect on Adulthood - CONCEPT Professional Training*. Concept.paloaltou.edu. https://concept.paloaltou.edu/resources/business-of-practice-blog/childhood-trauma

Novitsky, A. (2023, September 3). *The Fit Collective*. The Fit Collective. https://www.thefitcollective.com/blog/harnessing-the-power-of-grounding-techniques-for-emotional-regulation

Oswald, R. (2023, December 27). *Setting boundaries for well-being*. Mayo Clinic Health System. https://www.mayoclinichealthsystem.org/hometown-health/speaking-of-health/setting-boundaries-for-well-being

Raypole, C. (2020, November 13). *Emotional triggers: Definition and how to manage them*. Healthline. https://www.healthline.com/health/mental-health/emotional-triggers

Robinson, L., Smith, M., & Segal, J. (2018, November 3). *Emotional and Psychological Trauma - HelpGuide.org*. HelpGuide.org. https://www.helpguide.org/mental-health/ptsd-trauma/coping-with-emotional-and-psychological-trauma

Stuckey, H. L., & Nobel, J. (2010). *The Connection between Art, Healing, and Public Health: a Review of Current Literature*. American Journal of Public Health. https://doi.org/10.2105/ajph.2008.156497

Sweeney, A., Filson, B., Kennedy, A., Collinson, L., & Gillard, S. (2018, August 13). *A Paradigm shift: Relationships in trauma-informed Mental Health Services*. BJPsych Advances. https://doi.org/10.1192/bja.2018.29

3 breathing exercises to relieve stress. (2023). British Heart Foundation. https://www.bhf.org.uk/informationsupport/heart-matters-magazine/wellbeing/breathing-exercises

Tomeny, A. (2023, July 5). *Siv Counseling & Consultation*. Siv Counseling & Consultation. https://www.sivconsultation.com/blog/the-power-of-setting-boundaries-why-they-are-essential-for-personal-growth-and-well-being

Toussaint, L., Nguyen, Q. A., Roettger, C., Dixon, K., Offenbächer, M., Kohls, N., Hirsch, J., & Sirois, F. (2021). *Effectiveness of Progressive Muscle Relaxation, Deep Breathing, and Guided Imagery in Promoting Psychological and Physiological States of*

Relaxation (R. Taylor-Piliae, Ed.). Evidence-Based Complementary and Alternative Medicine. https://doi.org/10.1155/2021/5924040

Truitt, K. (2023, November 29). *The Healing Power of Art and Creative Expression in Trauma Recovery*. Trauma Counseling Center of Los Angeles. https://traumacounseling.com/trauma-therapy-blog/the-healing-power-of-art-and-creative-expression-in-trauma-recovery/

Understanding the Impact of Domestic Violence. (2023, April 17). Mclean Hospital. https://www.mcleanhospital.org/essential/domestic-violence

Unique Challenges of PTSD in Women. (2024, May 8). Bright Futures Treatment Center. https://brightfuturestreatment.com/unique-challenges-of-ptsd-in-women/

Book 3

Agents of Change. (2024, January 29). *What is Cognitive Processing Therapy?* Agents of Change Social Work Test Prep. https://agentsofchangeprep.com/blog/what-is-cognitive-processing-therapy-cpt/

Bay Area CBT Center. (2024, July 31). *The Synergy of Integrating EMDR and CBT*. Bay Area CBT Center. https://bayareacbtcenter.com/emdr-and-cbt-bilateral-stimulation-benefits/

Brandt, A. (2018). *9 Steps to Healing Childhood Trauma as an Adult*. Psychology Today. https://www.psychologytoday.com/us/blog/mindful-anger/201804/9-steps-healing-childhood-trauma-adult

Center. (2014). *Trauma-Specific Services*. Nih.gov; Substance Abuse and Mental Health Services Administration (US). https://www.ncbi.nlm.nih.gov/sites/books/NBK207184/

Chard, K. (2017). *Navigating Trauma Recovery: A Comparative Analysis of Cognitive Processing Therapy (CPT) and Eye Movement Desensitization and Reprocessing (EMDR)*. Pesi.com. https://www.pesi.com/blog/details/2220/navigating-trauma-recovery-a-comparative-analysis-of?srsltid=AfmBOopBhlyZTFPEqVHyyjxoQfTLrafW36rS_cJHaOPe5ryTz2lbExr9

Core Beliefs and Mental Health | HopeNation Counseling Services. (n.d.). Hopenationcounseling.com. https://hopenationcounseling.com/resources/core-beliefs

Dixon, L. B., Holoshitz, Y., & Nossel, I. (2016, February 1). *Treatment engagement of individuals experiencing mental illness: review and update*. World Psychiatry. https://doi.org/10.1002/wps.20306

Forlenza, S. (2024, February 7). *Summer Forlenza, LMFT | Online EMDR Therapy and EMDR Intensives*. Summer Forlenza, LMFT | Online EMDR Therapy and EMDR Intensives. https://www.summerforlenza.com/blog/memory-myths

From Self-Sabotage to Self-Love: Overcoming Negative Core Beliefs | Empower Counseling & Coaching. (2024, July 12). Empower Counseling & Coaching. https://empowercounselingllc.com/from-self-sabotage-to-self-love-overcoming-negative-core-beliefs/

Ken. (2024, May 18). RECO Intensive. https://recointensive.com/the-role-of-personalized-care-in-recovery-success/

M. Jan Holton, & Snodgrass, J. L. (2023, April 6). *A Theoretical and Theological Reframing of Trauma.* https://doi.org/10.1007/s11089-023-01063-1

Nurturing Emotional Well-Being: A Comprehensive Guide to DBT Self-Validation. (2024, March 18). The Counseling Center Group. https://counselingcentergroup.com/dbt-self-validation/

Peterson, I. (2022, May 17). *Visualizations and Affirmations.* Brain Energy Support Team. https://www.brainenergysupportteam.org/archives/37533

Phillips, L. (n.d.). *Tapping into the benefits of EMDR.* Www.counseling.org. https://www.counseling.org/publications/counseling-today-magazine/article-archive/article/legacy/tapping-into-the-benefits-of-emdr

Punamäki, R.-L., Qouta, S. R., & Peltonen, K. (2018, March 20). *Family systems approach to attachment relations, war trauma, and mental health among Palestinian children and parents.* European Journal of Psychotraumatology. https://doi.org/10.1080/20008198.2018.1439649

Resick, P. A., Nishith, P., Weaver, T. L., Astin, M. C., & Feuer, C. A. (2002). *A comparison of cognitive-processing therapy with prolonged exposure and a waiting condition for the treatment of chronic posttraumatic stress disorder in female rape victims.* Journal of Consulting and Clinical Psychology. https://doi.org/10.1037//0022-006x.70.4.867

Resnick, A. (2023, July 28). *How to Spot and Challenge Your Negative Core Beliefs, According to a Therapist.* Verywell Mind. https://www.verywellmind.com/how-to-challenge-your-negative-core-beliefs-7554706

Schaffner, A. (2020, June 26). *Identifying and Challenging Core Beliefs: 12 Helpful Worksheets.* PositivePsychology.com. https://positivepsychology.com/core-beliefs-worksheets/

Sorenson, S. (2024, March 11). *CBT vs. CPT: Understanding Their Roles in Psychological Healing.* Corner Canyon HC. https://cornercanyonhc.com/blog/cbt-vs-cpt/

Stanborough, R. J. (2023). *How to change negative thinking with cognitive restructuring.* Healthline. https://www.healthline.com/health/cognitive-restructuring

Using Polyvagal Theory, IFS, ACT, DBT & More to Treat Trauma, Anxiety & Depression. (2017). Pesi.com. https://catalog.pesi.com/sales/bh_c_022257_usingpolyvagalifsactdbt_organic-668419

Women's Issues. (2023, October). Center for Mindful Psychotherapy. https://mindfulcenter.org/womens-issues/

Wright, A. (2021, December 26). *An Inability To Visualize The Future (Let Alone A Positive Future) Is A Hallmark Of Trauma*. Annie Wright, LMFT. https://anniewright.com/inability-to-visualize-the-future-trauma/

Book 4

Bay Area CBT Center. (2024, July 22). *Rewire Your Brain with EMDR and Neuroplasticity*. Bay Area CBT Center. https://bayareacbtcenter.com/emdr-and-neuroplasticity/

EMDR therapy: What it is, procedure & effectiveness. (2022, March 29). Cleveland Clinic. https://my.clevelandclinic.org/health/treatments/22641-emdr-therapy

Everything You Need to Know About Using Eye Movement Desensitization and Reprocessing (EMDR) to Heal Trauma | All Points North. (2024, July 19). All Points North. https://apn.com/resources/emdr-heal-trauma/

Good, J. (2024, January 23). *GOOD EMDR THERAPY*. GOOD EMDR THERAPY. https://goodemdrtherapy.com/blog/how-to-find-the-best-emdr-therapist

The History of EMDR Therapy. (2024). EMDR Institute. https://www.emdr.com/history-of-emdr/

jewaldrop925. (2023, May 22). *How to choose an EMDR therapist | Mosaic Way Counseling*. Mosaic Way Counseling. https://mosaicwaycounseling.com/2023/05/22/how-to-choose-an-emdr-therapist/

Kaufman, S. (2021, August 13). *The eight phases of EMDR therapy*. EMDR International Association. https://www.emdria.org/blog/the-eight-phases-of-emdr-therapy/

Kaufman, S., & Melo, V. (2024, April 5). *Setting Client Expectations in EMDR Therapy*. EMDR International Association. https://www.emdria.org/blog/setting-client-expectations-in-emdr-therapy/

Key Techniques in EMDR Therapy Explained. (2024, September 19). Bay Area CBT Center. https://bayareacbtcenter.com/key-techniques-in-emdr-therapy-explained/

Lovering, N. (2022, May 9). *Neuroplasticity and Childhood Trauma: Effects, Healing, and EMDR*. Psych Central. https://psychcentral.com/ptsd/the-roles-neuroplasticity-and-emdr-play-in-healing-from-childhood-trauma

Mentalmaptowellness. (2024, December 4). *EMDR for Trauma: A Life-Changing Approach*. MentalMaptoWellness. https://www.mentalmaptowellness.com/post/emdr-for-trauma-a-life-changing-approach

Miller, K. D. (2019, July 2). *Fourteen health benefits of practicing gratitude according to science*. Positive Psychology. https://positivepsychology.com/benefits-of-gratitude/

Raypole, C. (2024, January 29). *30 grounding techniques to quiet distressing thoughts*. Healthline. https://www.healthline.com/health/grounding-techniques

Shapiro, F. (2014). *The role of eye movement desensitization and reprocessing (EMDR) therapy in medicine: Addressing the psychological and physical symptoms stemming from adverse life experience*. The Permanente Journal; National Library of Medicine. https://doi.org/10.7812/tpp/13-098

Wetherford, R. (n.d.). Francine Shapiro EMDR Interview. Www.psychotherapy.net. https://www.psychotherapy.net/interview/francine-shapiro-emdr

Zamudio, N. (2024a). Ascension Counseling & Therapy. https://ascensioncounseling.com/9-effective-methods-for-reducing-trauma-related-hyperarousal

Zamudio, N. (2024b). Ascension Counseling & Therapy. https://ascensioncounseling.com/emdr-therapy-techniques

Zamudio, N. (2024c). Ascension Counseling & Therapy. https://ascensioncounseling.com/emdr-therapy-techniques-for-unraveling-generational-trauma

Book 5

Benefits Of Exercise For Mental Health In Adults. (2024, November 6). Mental Health Center of San Diego. https://mhcsandiego.com/blog/benefits-exercise-mental-health-adults/

CFI Team. (2022). *SMART Goals*. Corporate Finance Institute; CFI. https://corporatefinanceinstitute.com/resources/management/smart-goal/

Cherry, K. (2023). *How Some People Are More Resilient When It Comes to Stress*. Verywell Mind. https://www.verywellmind.com/characteristics-of-resilience-2795062

DeJurnett, K. (2024, July 15). *This Mental Health Technique Takes Effort and Commitment to Yield the Best Results (Like Most Things)*. Medium. https://medium.com/@christelclear/this-mental-health-technique-takes-effort-and-commitment-to-yield-the-best-results-like-most-2a6083285513

Derenale-Betti, D. (2024, August 21). *Resilient People: 10 Traits of Highly Resilient People - #hersmile*. #Hersmile. https://hersmile.org/resilient-people-10-traits/

Find a Support Group or Local Program. (2023, January 17). Www.samhsa.gov. https://www.samhsa.gov/find-support/health-care-or-support/support-group-or-local-program

Gunton, A. V. (2024, September 16). *Exercise & Mental Health: How Movement Affects Emotions*. New Horizons Medical. https://newhorizonsmedical.org/2024/09/exercise-mental-health-how-movement-affects-emotions/

Journaling for Mental Health. (2019). University of Rochester Medical Center. https://www.urmc.rochester.edu/encyclopedia/content.aspx?ContentID=4552&ContentTypeID=1

Journaling to increase self-awareness. (n.d.). Prosper. https://prosper.liverpool.ac.uk/postdoc-resources/reflect/journaling-to-increase-self-awareness/

Keng, S. L., Smoski, M. J., & Robins, C. J. (2011). *Effects of Mindfulness on Psychological health: a Review of Empirical Studies*. Clinical Psychology Review. https://doi.org/10.1016/j.cpr.2011.04.006

Kim & Hill. (2010, July 21). *Neural Plasticity: 4 Steps to Change Your Brain & Habits*. Authenticity Associates; Authenticity Associates. https://www.authenticityassociates.com/neural-plasticity-4-steps-to-change-your-brain/

Lachance, L., & Ramsey, D. (2015, March). *Food, Mood, and Brain Health: Implications for the Modern Clinician*. Missouri Medicine. https://pmc.ncbi.nlm.nih.gov/articles/PMC6170050/

Lavender, D. (2023, June 21). *The Healing Effects of Mindfulness on Mental Health | Camino Recovery Spain*. Camino Recovery Spain. https://www.caminorecovery.com/blog/healing-effects-of-mindfulness-on-mental-health/

Ma, C., Qirui, C., & Lv, Y. (2023, December 14). *"One community at a time": promoting community resilience in the face of natural hazards and public health challenges*. BMC Public Health; BioMed Central. https://doi.org/10.1186/s12889-023-17458-x

Perry, E. (2025). *Life planning: The ultimate guide (and template) to transform your life*. Betterup.com. https://www.betterup.com/blog/life-planning

Selhub, E. (2022, September 18). Nutritional psychiatry: Your brain on food. Harvard Health Blog. https://www.health.harvard.edu/blog/nutritional-psychiatry-your-brain-on-food-201511168626

Taking Steps to Rewire the Brain. (2020, January 24). Khiron Clinics. https://khironclinics.com/blog/taking-steps-to-rewire-the-brain/

Vorecol Editorial Team. (2024). *What Psychological Techniques Can Help Align Personal Ambitions with Company Goals?*. Vorecol.com. https://vorecol.com/blogs/blog-what-psychological-techniques-can-help-align-personal-ambitions-with-company-goals-204453

What Is Community Resilience and Why Does It matter? (2024). UrbanFootprint. https://urbanfootprint.com/community-resilience-meaning/

Wright, K. W. (2023, June 29). *Vision Board: Ideas & Tips to Inspire Your Goals*. Day One | Your Journal for Life. https://dayoneapp.com/blog/vision-board/

Zeine, F., Jafari, N., Nami, M., & Blum, K. (2024, March 1). *Awareness Integration Theory A Psychological and Genetic Path to Self-Directed Neuroplasticity*. Health Sciences Review (Oxford); Elsevier BV. https://doi.org/10.1016/j.hsr.2024.100169

Made in the USA
Columbia, SC
17 June 2025